THROWING IN THE TOWEL

BEN DOUGHTY

Copyright© 2021 Ben Doughty
All rights reserved

No part of this book may be reproduced, or stored in a retrieval system, or transmitted in any form or by any means, electronic, mechanical, photocopying, recording, or otherwise without express written permission of the publisher.

Cover designed: Julian McGowan
Editor: Natalie Bleau

This book is dedicated to the memory of Tony .Burns MBE. A true Eastend Legend

Chris,

Thanks for your support, always

Ben Douglas

1/ LAST EXIT FROM BROOKLYN

After the fight, it didn't take long for things to go pear shaped with the crazy naked black chick. For my part, I could probably have soldiered on but as July gave way to August, Nicquae had gotten on Kat's last nerve. Accordingly - and no doubt emboldened by her daily intake of budget malt liquor - she resolved to speak her mind one evening on the matter of domestic unrest.

"You're bonkers aren't you...?" said Kat in a tone more consistent with pronouncement than enquiry. As if to prove the accusation beyond any reasonable doubt, Nicquae immediately went berserk, screaming, "I'M NOT CRAZY...! I'M NOT CRAZY...! I'M JUST NOT USED TO MY MEDS..."

Upon hearing the kerfuffle in the next room, I thought it best to arbitrate. I entered the large bedroom cum lounge area that Niquae had selfishly commandeered on the day we moved in and stood firm with my drunken girlfriend. Things were not working out and being as there were two of us and only one of her, she ought to be the one to leave graciously, I argued. Niquae wasn't having it:

"No, I would like to stay, please," she insisted whilst wiping the tears from her eyes. The three of us moving in together had been a lamentable mistake and now there loomed a custody battle for our Sunset Park abode. Clearly, it wasn't something that could be settled without protraction, so Kat and I retired to our designated bedroom whilst Niquae screamed down the phone at her NYPD boyfriend in order to bring him up to speed with developments. At least we could be reasonably confident that she wouldn't attempt to get into bed with us tonight as she had done on previous occasions. Niquae was cute but she was also certifiably nuts and that is always a deal breaker.

Within a couple of days, Kat and I decided to throw in the towel and return to London. It wasn't an easy decision as I was firmly entrenched at Gleason's and scheduled to turn pro under Moe's tutelage and guidance. Once again, my whole identity was wrapped up in the idea of being a fighter and it was something that only seemed real in New York. It was where I had sparred with the champs and emerged the moral victor in a statistically unsuccessful comeback fight. Having proven myself in Brooklyn and garnered a degree of credibility at one of the most famous gyms in the world, I wasn't looking forward to starting from scratch back in London. Gleason's Gym was a pugilistic melting pot that transcended colour, creed or gender and simply demanded an entry level quota of bottle and guile. I wasn't at all sure if an equivalent could be found back home.

At the same time, I missed London Town and was about ready to come up for air. I was looking forward to seeing my friends and, vainglorious as ever, I was especially keen to show off my newly ripped physique. Unfortunately, my proudly chiselled torso would be a painful shade of scarlet by the time I landed on English soil due to a booze assisted nap on Cammy's sun roof, shortly before we flew home. We spent our last few days in NY as her guest in the shoe box sized apartment on the Upper West Side and our brief tenure was not entirely without incident. Kat pretty much despised Cammy due to our fleeting sexual history and, consequently, her behaviour was even more truculent than one might have expected under normal circumstances. Her 'piece de resistance' was apparently faking an epileptic style fit on a Saturday night after a mandatory skinful of wine and beer. We were sufficiently concerned to call an Ambulance but when a pair of Afro-Caribbean paramedics - a man and a woman - arrived on the scene, Kat miraculously rose from her trembling languor and declared, "You don't work for the Ambulance company…You're the people who stop Christina Aguilera from getting her arse kicked…!" Presumably, she thought they resembled security guards.

Upon landing at Heathrow, we took a taxi all the way back to Clerkenwell at the expense of Kat's Mum. It was a blatant extravagance justified on the basis that my sunburned skin was too tender to be subjected to the discomfort of carrying heavy luggage on London Transport. Sitting in the back of the cab, I gazed at the convoy of quintessentially English traffic and the quaint anomaly of Hatton Cross Roundabout with patriotic affection. Returning to one's natural habitat after an extended period abroad can be profoundly surrealistic and even the humble Esso garage seemed to take on the beauty and significance of the Taj Mahal.

An hour later, the cab pulled up on Sekforde Street where we were greeted by Kats Mum who was as profusely nice as ever. She remarked that I looked 'lean' and had been 'very brave' to have that fight in New York. Shortly before leaving, I had hated London and everything it seemed to stand for in the 21st century but - with my rediscovered mojo - it felt good to be back.

After a week of pissed up revelry and reunion with Ed and the usual suspects, my first priority was to find a gym. On that account, Kat and I took a trip one afternoon to Maloney's Fight Factory on the Old Kent

Road, situated on the site where the Henry Cooper pub and gymnasium had once stood. The Guvnor was Eugene Maloney - brother of Frank - who briefly had a presence on the UK fight scene as a promoter and manager before disappearing a few years later amid rumours of gambling debts to unforgiving creditors. As we entered the predictably claustrophobic gym on the first floor of the building, veteran trainer Alan Smith was winding up a session with a new lightweight signing. When he ordered his charge to do a round of skipping by way of a cool down, I introduced myself.

"What's the crack with using the gym...? I've been training for 6 months at Gleason's in New York and I'm looking for some decent sparring."

He eyed me suspiciously but said nothing.

"I've had 35 amateur fights and was thinking about turning pro."

"IF we need you for sparring, "he shot back with visible scepticism. "Most amateurs are no good to us whatsoever."

It was obvious that he took me for one of those random flakes off the street who nurse dreams of being a prizefighter despite the inability to distinguish a left hook from a fishhook. With a degree of indignation, I told him:

"Well, I've been sparring with Vivian Harris, the WBA light welterweight champion and I did ok with him."

Mr Smith was unimpressed.

"We've got good sparring already, with the likes of Wayne Elcock... the world champion...."

"WBU Champion...!" I corrected him. "C'mon, you're talking about an 11-fight novice. All I'm saying is that I can give anyone a workout."

My lack of regard for the WBU strap seemed to give me a flicker of momentum as he suddenly asked, "How old are you...?"

"33..."

"Ahh... we wouldn't sign anyone who's 33. And if you can't sell a hundred tickets then you wouldn't get on a show. That's boxing as a business."

A hundred tickets…? Harry Burgess had never said anything about selling tickets. Then again, Harry was no longer a force and the legendary Thomas A' Becket was now an Estate Agents. On balance, I'd probably have stood a better chance convincing an estate agent that I knew my way around the ring. Despite the recently flattened proboscis, I just didn't look like a boxer. Certainly not to Alan Smith's practiced eye.

"Come back when Eugene the manager is here and have a word with him," he suggested.

I thanked the man for his time and motioned to Kat that we were leaving. Back on the street, my low expectations confirmed, I already knew I wouldn't be going back. The Fight Factory would go belly up a few years later, in any case, as the old school gym above a boozer became an antiquated phenomenon. I still see Alan Smith on the scene today but if he remembers our fruitless conversation in the summer of 2003 then he's never mentioned it.

2/ ANGEL DELIGHT

My next port of call was the Kronk. Not to be confused with the iconic Detroit original, Kronk St Pancras had been launched 3 years earlier in a blaze of publicity with Thomas Hearns and Manny Steward on hand to endorse the London franchise. It was a large facility opposite Talacre Park in Kentish Town with an ABA club and a commercial pro gym operating under the same roof. Working on reception was a young Nigerian amateur that I would come to know as Larry Ekundayo. I gave him the same pitch I'd given to Alan Smith, and he was considerably more hospitable. He'd had over 50 amateur fights he told me and had only gotten the short end on 2 occasions. Since he was a welterweight, I suggested we might do a bit of sparring at some point. He nodded to signify that it wouldn't be a problem. With his perfectly proportioned ebony frame, he probably fancied his chances against a bloke with a Brit Pop haircut and a 1970s red Adidas tracksuit top. After getting the lowdown on gym fees and membership, I vowed to return although I never did. 6 months later, Larry and I would come within one fight of meeting each other in the Northwest Divs.

I would likely have gone back to the Kronk had Kat's Mum not noticed that there was a boxing club on St John Street near the college where she taught foreign students. She wasn't sure if it was 'just for kids' but being a stone's throw from the house it seemed worthy of investigation. In the spirit of nothing ventured - nothing gained, I took a stroll to Islington and Finsbury Youth Club on Owens Row on a cool Thursday evening unsure of whether it would be open during the summer hiatus. I walked through a wrought iron gate, down some steps leading to a two-storey building with a laminated sign on the door bearing the logo 'ANGEL AMATEUR BOXING CLUB.' The door was locked and there were no audible signs of life inside. I was about to leave when a bespectacled elderly gentleman wearing beige slacks and a navy-blue blazer came ambling down the steps with methodical caution.

"Hello, sir. Are you connected to the boxing club...?"

"I'm John Jacobs, competition secretary," he announced with the kind of luminous pride one might reserve for being named in the Queen's honours list. "Do you know, we're a very famous club...?"

Aware that he was somewhat exaggerating, I played along in the interests of diplomacy. "Oh yeah.... Everybody's heard of the Angel ABC.... I've had 35 bouts and I was looking for somewhere to...."

"How OLD are you...?"

"33."

"You're too old...!"

I tried a different tack. "Well, I'd be up for helping the lads with their training, regardless..."

"Now, that's a different matter," he replied "We are always looking for trainers. Come in and I'll show you around the gym."

Groping for the requisite key in that painstakingly tortuous way that old people seem to do everything, he eventually opened the door and ushered me inside. On the ground floor was a small office and an adjacent room containing a 12-foot ring, chiefly designated for junior sparring, he explained. The upper floor consisted of a large area adorned with numerous punchbags and an adjoining room that housed a 16-foot ring for senior sparring. Noticeably, there were no pictures of former luminaries or other symbols of success displayed on the walls. Despite the absence of memorabilia, there was something about the place that fired my imagination, and I experienced a rush of excitement at the thought of mentoring young boxers and moulding them in my own image. Being 'too old' for the cutting edge, perhaps this could be my legacy.

"We start back for the new season next Tuesday at 6 O' clock," said John Jacobs. "Come as you are, and I'll introduce you to the other trainers." Strangely, he saw fit to add, "Bring a towel..."

"No problem, John. Look forward to seeing you next week." I thought it best to provide the old boy with an escort off the premises lest he should fall prey to one of more notorious local gangs, delineated by the names of the housing estates they came from. Admittedly - if he were to be accosted by the dregs of Islington's disenfranchised youth - there seemed a genuine possibility he might bore them to death. I don't recall asking for specifics but, suddenly, he informed me that he was 83 years old. Disparaging quips aside, you had to hand it to him. The Angel ABC was clearly his lifeblood. I walked my new octogenarian pal to his beige Austin Metro and concluded that it had been a good day.

I returned the following Tuesday at 5.30pm and found Mr. Jacobs seated behind his desk in the office. Upon my arrival, he took me upstairs and introduced me to a big, shaven headed mixed-race guy with an athletic build and prominent facial scarring.

"Duncan, this is Ben. He'll be coming to us as a trainer..."

Duncan looked a little hesitant before offering his hand and saying, "Ok, mate... Doesn't take long to pick it up..."

It seemed an inherently odd thing to say, especially since he had no awareness of my previous experience. Considering it a mild affront, I asked him, "What's your background in the game...?"

"No background, "he replied, "I'm just a shit hot personal trainer....!"

His tone was defensive and any credibility he might have had in my eyes essentially withered and died on the spot. Within 20 minutes, the gym had marginally filled up with 6-8 young lads aged between 11 and 16, talking amongst themselves whilst getting changed in readiness for the session. Over the years, the club had produced a few champions, most notably PJ and Patrick Gallagher but in September 2003 the 'squad' was sufficiently threadbare to make any utilisation of the downstairs gym unnecessary. A little ginger kid turned on a ghetto blaster tuned to some popular radio station and Duncan instructed the boys to shadow box. They were all raw novices but the standout was a stocky, dark haired southpaw by the name of John Ryder who had an air of quiet confidence and self-possession.

After 3 rounds of shadow boxing, the order came to partner up and practice blocking one another's jabs as the dulcet tones of Jamelia engulfed the gym. By way of breaking the ice, I made myself useful, correcting faults and offering advice. It was obvious that Duncan was an enthusiastic fitness trainer without too much technical know-how but equally apparent that he saw himself as the Guvnor and might not take kindly to another strong personality who had been there and done it to some extent. Midway through the session, a gregarious character called Alfie entered the proceedings. He was my age and had boxed for the club during his teenage years before becoming a trainer. He greeted me warmly and immediately asked,

"Did you box, mate...? How many did you have...?"

"35, "I told him. "But only one in the last 15 years... In New York a few weeks ago, as it goes..."

Most ex - boxers have an instinctive kinship and I liked him immediately. So far as I could gather, he was the official head coach but - being a free spirit - his sporadic attendance had effectively allowed Duncan to assume pole position. At the tender age of 33 - having walked an alternative path in life - I was still somewhat naive about the machinations of 'office politics and one-upmanship. Added to the fact that diplomacy wasn't my strong suit, Duncan and I would lock horns frequently in the next several months. Inevitably, I came to see him as the malign influence, but the simple fact was that we both wanted the same thing. Above and beyond the joys of 'giving back', I was looking for a vehicle but would need to loosen his grip on the steering wheel. Before long, I realised that Alfie merely wanted a quiet life but was torn between natural laziness and a sentimental attachment to the club and its members.

At the end of the night, the 3 of us held a quick conference in the trainer's office and agreed that the club would open on Tuesday, Thursday and Friday evenings plus Saturday mornings. "Not gonna' get any champions opening 2 nights a week are we...?" reasoned Alfie. My first night as a coach and here I was involved in the major decision-making process already. It seemed like heady stuff.

Cutting my teeth in this new role, I was soon sparring with the boys, especially John Ryder who was too strong and advanced for the other lads anywhere near his age and weight. Despite being 15 years old, he punched like a man and had obvious potential that had clearly been stagnating under the existing regime. John Jacobs had a reputation on the circuit as being a difficult man to deal with and was terribly hesitant to put boys out on shows which probably explained why there were so few boxers when I came on board. After watching the two of us move around one evening, Alfie took me to one side:

"You're not bad, although you do hang your chin out. Don't you still want to fight...?"

"I do but John said I'm too old, "I replied.

He shook his head. "Bollocks...! We've hardly got any boxers. If he doesn't put you out, then he's wasting you. I'll have a word with him...."

Whatever he said must have resonated because Mr. Jacobs was soon in favour of getting me 'carded' and asked me to bring in my USA Boxing license so he could send it to the London ABA in support of an application. A week later, a new medical card turned up bearing my name, despite the abject lack of a mandatory examination. Whomever it may have concerned had simply taken the passport sized photograph from my American card and inserted it into the freshly issued ME3 with a rubber stamp. The old curmudgeon may have been difficult to get along with, but he evidently had a bit of clout with ABA top brass. I was now ready to resume my career although matching me wouldn't be easy, he sagely warned.

"They're going to think, '35 bouts in America… He must have come up the hard way…'"

I tried to explain that I'd only had one bout in America and lost but it didn't seem to register. From my perspective it was immaterial. He could match me with Godzilla for all I cared.

For the next couple of weeks, I divided my time at the gym between training myself and coaching the lads until, one afternoon, Mr. Jacobs called to say that he had a fight for me vs one Luke Calvert of Finchley ABC. Calvert was a 2-time National Junior Champion with 38 wins from 52 contests but this would be the 18 year old's first senior bout. I genuinely didn't care who I fought and was happy to sign off, but Alfie voiced his misgivings in the office that same evening.

"Double ABA champion, 52 bouts…! Are you sure about this…? He might be a right banger…."

His protective instincts were tantamount to an insult and drew my indignant retort:

"I don't give a fuck what he might be. I have got one hell of a chin and I know my way around that ring…!"

Alfie smiled and turned to young John Ryder who was also matched on the show in question.

"You see, John…? This is what you've gotta be like…!"

The match was made for Friday October 17 at the Shen Ola Banqueting Suite in Hackney. If I'd bitten off more than I could chew then we would find out soon enough.

3/ THE FIRST CUT IS THE DEEPEST

I left Kat on her 22nd birthday because it just wasn't working anymore. We'd never had a traditional boyfriend/ girlfriend dynamic to begin with but had proved a reasonably good fit during times of aimless gallivanting. Now that I had goals and a new sense of mission, the relationship seemed untenable, as did the whole 'regime' at Sekforde Street. I was hardly a born-again teetotaller but Kat's routine was hugely non conducive to any kind of training ethos, hence she continued to drink herself into a nightly stupor without my participation or support. As I attempted to live monastically, she would frequently go out on her own before returning several hours later, hammered and obnoxious, the resentments of a woman scorned looming large. It had gotten to the point where I couldn't stand the sight of her after 8pm. It wasn't her fault, but the time had come for an emergency exit plan.

Accordingly, I found myself a room above 'The Green Man' on Essex Road for £80 a week. The landlord was a balding, bespectacled Irish bloke who seemed constantly overworked and quietly aggrieved about his station in life. Regardless, he was only asking for one week's deposit and a week's rent up front which was just as well, given the constant state of penury in which I existed. I was still working on the phones at I.F.F in order to earn a crust which meant that I continued to see Kat on a regular basis. The room was pokey, and the pub would have passed for rough but it suited my idea of the Spartan surroundings necessary for fistic excellence. Over the years, I'd read innumerable accounts of fighters locking themselves away in similarly squalid accommodations and concluded that luxury was the enemy.

With a week to go until the fight, I squeezed in a couple more sparring sessions with John Ryder before giving him a pep talk about the pressures of making one's amateur debut and the need to focus on what we had practiced in the gym. He was an extremely likeable kid, and I was already nursing visions of him turning over and becoming my first world champion one day. I had a lot to learn about the business but, 16 years later, only a trio of myopic judges would prevent John from fulfilling such lofty expectations at this time of writing.

I felt a strong sense of deja vu, climbing into the back of the club minibus at 5pm on a Friday evening with Ed and Jenny in tow. The event was a dinner show, hence not open to the general public, but I was told that I could bring 2 guests. With the ugliness of our breakup in the rear-view mirror, Jenny and I had made up a couple of years earlier and were good platonic friends once more. Ed, with his natural fear of 'chavs', wasn't sure what to expect from the excursion but was too loyal to decline such an invitation. Also seated in the back of the vehicle were John Ryder and his brother-in-law, the landlord of a nearby pub and 3 young boxers from the Angel, along for their first taste of a live show. In the front sat John Jacobs, Alfie and Duncan, the designated driver.

The venue was only 25 minutes away, but our progress was marginally slowed by an accident on Hackney Road, apparently involving a teenager on a bike. With police and ambulance services on the scene, Alfie suddenly leaned out of the window and shouted, "MURDERER...!" in a dark, inappropriate parody of the song 'Here Comes The Hotstepper." The butterflies in my stomach and gallows humour made me feel 18 again.

When we arrived at the large ballroom on Waterden Road, Luke Calvert - who was still 18 for the first time - could scarcely believe that I was his opponent. Although my nose had been flattened by world class pros in New York, I still looked like someone who might have failed an audition for 'These Animal Men.' Not to be thrown off the scent, I heard his coach whisper conspiratorially, "I bet you that's him...." With it being a Finchley ABC show, they might normally have enjoyed the luxury of a home changing room but, on this occasion, a curtain had been drawn at the back of the hall with all boxers and teams lumped in together. Ryder was on third and I was due in straight afterwards.

John lost a close, debatable decision to another debutant from All Stars with an impressively unpronounceable Greek surname. Clearly dreading such an eventuality, the old boy retained as Master of Ceremonies self-consciously announced the winner as "IN THE RED.....CHATTANOOGA CHOO-CHOO..!"
On a different night, I might have found it comical, but nothing seems funny when you are walking to the ring, suddenly longing to be a member of the audience, anonymous and safe. I gave my club mate a consolatory glove tap as I mounted the steps, hoping to give the Angel mob something to cheer about.

The bell sounded for the first round, and I proceeded to get hit more times than East London in the Blitz. It was as if I had frozen momentarily and didn't expect the kid to come so quickly out of the traps. He had an impressive variety and nailed me with several unanswered punches before I returned fire and drove him back across the ring. The barrage seemed to wake me up as I began to time his attacks which were suddenly finding nothing besides fresh air. I felt the ring rust eroding and finished the round on equal terms, but it had been a bad start, all the same. When I got back to the corner, Alfie had a sanguine view of the proceedings.

"Well done, Ben. I think you're on top, mate…"

I was far from convinced but still found the words encouraging. I did better still in the second round but picked up a standing count which annoyed me as I wasn't hurt in the slightest. As the referee tolled on his fingers, I briefly contemplated what had become of a once manly pursuit. Head guards and standing 8 counts were for pussies as far as I was concerned, and I'd taken a much harder shot earlier in the round that had me hearing bells. Would such mollycoddling eventually result in fights being stopped due to broken eyelashes…?

I was coming on strong in the third, when he landed a blow that caused my head guard to move which - in turn - opened a cut in the corner of my right eye. Unaware of where the blood was coming from, I bitterly protested as the fight was waved off with around 30 seconds remaining but referee, Billy Phillips, was having none of it. "That's a stitches job," he opined gravely, "Live to fight another day, son."

As I walked back to the changing area, Finchley matchmaker, Johnny Ball, slapped me on the back vociferously and said I had done "Fucking brilliant." for a man with only one bout since the Teletext era. John Jacobs agreed: "That was maturing into a win for you. We'll have the return on our show." Surprisingly, I felt elated despite the result. A year ago, there seemed to be more chance of me splitting the atom than returning to the ring, but I had just acquitted myself well against a champion almost half my age. I was of the opinion that I had earned a drink at the very least.

Thankfully, John Ryder's brother-in-law had brought some cans of lager along with a camcorder on which he had filmed the night's action. At only 4 percent volume, Foster's wouldn't have been my tipple of choice, but it was better than nothing and I downed the first can before even getting changed. After the paramedics had given me the once over and fixed some butterfly strips to my eye, the entourage gathered itself together and headed back to the car park for post-mortems and commiseration. Although we had both lost, the atmosphere was upbeat if not positively triumphal. And little Ginger Jake said I've have won if the ring had been bigger.

Less than an hour later, I was in the familiar ambience of The Good Mixer with Ed and Jen, toasting my heroic failure with several pints of Kronenbourg and shots of Jack Daniels. "Even if it hadn't been stopped, I think he would have won," said Jenny who was never one to let a friendship get in the way of the truth. At throwing out time, we caught the Tube back to Angel and holed up in my room with the obligatory kebabs and a cheap bottle of scotch. I hadn't touched a drop for 3 whole weeks before the fight and intended to make up for it with a vengeance, but my tolerance had lowered sufficiently for me to pass out before midnight.

I woke up the next morning - still half drunk - to find Jenny on the other side of the bed and Ed sprawled on the floor. Roused into action by mischievous prodding, he and I were soon swigging whisky from the shiny silver cup I had 'won' the night before as I suggested we pay a visit to the gym. I was basically seeking congratulation for my efforts of 12 hours earlier but one of them should have told me it was a bad idea.

Jenny left for work while Ed and I had a few more shots of scotch before freshening up and catching the 38 bus to Goswell Road, a short walk from the gym. Upon arrival, I changed into the copiously bloodstained kit I had worn the previous evening and ventured upstairs to find Duncan in mid-session with half a dozen of the lads. I was high as a kite by now and asked if anyone wanted to spar, the stitches over my eye notwithstanding. Duncan looked vaguely perturbed and gently asked, "Have you had a drink, Ben...?"

"Just a hair of the dog, " I shrugged.

"Yeah, I thought so. I think you'd better go home and come back next week, mate. Not a good look when there's kids around."

A few months down the line he would likely have used the incident as ammunition, but it was early days and we had yet to reach the 'Cold War' stage. The frightening thing was my genuine lack of suspicion that turning up at a youth club covered in blood and wreaking of whisky was not the most appropriate comportment for a community sports coach. Today, it seems unimaginable but at the time I had no idea how to live within the confines of society's accepted norms.

4/ WEMBLEY

The following week at the gym, enthused by my performance against Calvert, John Jacobs asked if I wanted to enter the Senior ABA Championships. It was tantamount to asking a bear if he was in the habit defecating outdoors. Somewhat jumping the gun, I asked, "If I win it, would that put me in the mix for the Olympics next year...?"

He grinned broadly and said, "I like your confidence but let's worry about the Northwest Divs first...! I'll get you an application form and ask Jack Danbury for the dates."

That I could even ask such a question was proof in itself of how long I'd been off the scene. By the 21st century, the ABA title had lost much of its former prestige and wining it was irrelevant to the selection process for major international tournaments. It was commonplace for elite amateurs to swerve the national championships altogether in favour of various qualifiers all over the world in an effort to secure their places in the Commonwealth Games, The Worlds or the Olympics due to be held in Athens the following Summer. Obviously, the weakened field made it easier to win a national title, but I'd have taken no pleasure in such logic. I had an all or nothing mentality and - after years of doing nothing - I suddenly wanted it all.

There was, however, a potential stumbling block in the shape of good old-fashioned bureaucracy. The international governing body for amateur boxing had recently lowered the upper age limit to 34, meaning that I would be ineligible for competition as of February 2004. Having received the tournament schedule, Mr. Jacobs called me into the office one night and asked, "When's your birthday...?"

"February 4th," I replied.

"Well then you're buggered...! The Northwest Divs are on February 5th..."

I experienced a sinking feeling, having set my heart on one last quest for glory, when he put on his glasses and plucked my medical card from his inside blazer pocket. He turned to the first page and frowned for a moment before saying, "Wait a second... You don't know your own birthday...! It says April 2nd here..."
I leaned across the desk and studied the text underneath the passport sized photograph that read: 'D.O.B: 02/04/1970...' It appeared that the American practice of recording the date backwards had worked in my favour. As my card had been fast tracked, the administrator had

clearly copied the digits exactly as they appeared on my USA licence, making me 2 months younger as far as the ABA were concerned. I tried to explain the anomaly to Mr. Jacobs, but he remained steadfast in his belief that I was simply unaware of the date on which I had entered this mortal coil.

With his characteristic penchant for overkill, he summoned me upstairs and interrupted the training session to announce that I would be representing the club in the championships next year and implored all sundry to get behind me for the greater good. Having previously been 'too old', I was now Angel ABC's flagship fighter. Our leader also had good relations with the press and had gotten me a few flattering write ups in the Islington Gazette and other periodicals off the back of the Calvert loss. One local rag described me as 'the 33-year-old fighter who has recently returned from New York...' Starting to believe the hype, I was suddenly obsessed with my goal of becoming ABA Welterweight Champion, 2004. It was all that mattered.

Perhaps, I should say it was almost all that mattered. I was ticking over in the gym but being as the 'Divs' were 14 weeks away I had pretty much set aside the month of December for the purpose of drinking and generally enjoying the Christmas break. The plan was to get it all out of my system before knuckling down to serious training as of January 1st. Back at Gleason's, Paulie Mallignaggi had once told me that he didn't drink - or indulge in sexual activity - for 5 weeks before a fight. Since it seemed to be working out well for him, I decided to adopt the same blueprint. I didn't have a lady in my life or any semblance of a 'booty call' at the time so the secondary clause would merely involve abstaining from masturbation. I didn't anticipate too much difficulty in observing said sacrifice and was hoping to acquire the explosive meanness of a peak Sonny Liston as a result.

With my immediate future mapped out accordingly, 2003 culminated in a trip to Brighton on New Year's Eve with Ed and the boys. I was planning to stay at the house of a girl Ed was seeing but ended up pulling a young lady whilst out on the town and woke up the next morning in the Seven Dials area. I was chronically hung over in the way that turns even a fleeting trip to the bathroom into a head spinning ordeal but felt marginally better after my hostess had fixed me a toasted sausage sandwich. I took her number before saying goodbye but somehow managed to lose it thus scuppering any possibility of further romance. In any case, I had told her that I would be unavailable for the next 5 weeks at least.

Back in London for the first week of January, I made my way to the legendary Repton Boxing Club in Bethnal Green in search of decent sparring. If I was to do myself any kind of justice whatsoever in the ABAs then I needed to get some rounds in with more accomplished and experienced boxers than could be found at the Angel, where John Ryder was my only credible option. As good a prospect as he was, he was still a junior novice and a southpaw at that. Since John Jacobs seemed to regard inter - club sparring as only slightly less taboo than maternal incest, my expedition would need to be a covert one.

It was a Friday evening when I first walked through the hallowed portals of the old Victorian Bath House on Cheshire Street and the scene, I encountered could genuinely have been mocked up for a British gangster movie. The near side apron of the large, elevated ring was lined with middle aged men who all seemed to be smoking and flicking the ash into saucers as they collectively focussed on the action inside the ropes. It was a buzzing hive of activity that reminded me of the gym scenes in 'Rocky' transplanted onto an East End backdrop. I asked who might be in charge and the smoking crew all pointed in unison to a squat imposing figure with matted grey hair, wearing green track suit bottoms and a dark blue body warmer. I already knew his name, of course, but this was the first time I had seen the amateur boxing deity known as Tony Burns in the flesh. As I approached, he fixed me with an unblinking stare by way of a mute invitation to state my business.

"Hello... I've come here because I'm looking for some good sparring...."

His eyes continued to scrutinise mine, but he said nothing.

"Erm. Have you have heard of Luke Calvert...?"

He nodded and widened his eyes in what I took to be a sardonic expression of awe.

"Well, I boxed him in my last fight..."

"Did you win...?" he wanted to know.

"No, I got stopped on a cut eye, but it was close before they stopped it..."

"WAS IT...?" (Still sardonic.)

"Yeah... It was."

"Get changed...!" he ordered.

Sensing that time was at a premium, I darted into 'The World-Famous Repton Changing Room' and hurriedly put my kit on. When I returned, Tony Burns walked over to a tall, dark-haired fighter and instructed him to, "Glove up, son..." Obediently, his charge donned a head guard and gloves before mounting the steps and ducking through the ropes. Expecting a standard warm up, I had begun to shadow box in the large mirror when my flow was interrupted by the words, "Alright Rocky, whenever you're ready...?"

Unsure if he was referring to me, I looked at him quizzically.

"You wanted to spar didn't you...?" snapped Tony Burns.

"Yeah..."

"Well get up there then...!"

I put on my own head guard and gloves without assistance and clambered into the 20ft ring with its distinctive mint green canvas. Still feeling a little 'tight', I bounced on the balls of my feet for a few seconds until Mr. Burns commanded, "OFF YA' GO...."

My sparring partner - whom I suspected to be reigning ABA welterweight champion, Danny Happe - was a very smooth, clever southpaw. The style was quintessentially amateur, but he was obviously an elite operator within the confines of 3 or 4 rounds. He boxed with aplomb rather than swagger and was particularly adept at pushing away off his lead foot whenever I threw a jab. But I seemed to be holding my own when the supremo called, "TIME...!" to signal the end of the first round. I had to ask:

"Are you Danny Happe...?"

"Yeah...!" he smiled, seemingly grateful for the recognition.

We boxed another two rounds before the head coach decreed, "That's enough..." and motioned for us to vacate the ring. Buzzing to have moved around with an A list fighter in such an iconic building, I bombarded the two of them with questions once back on the gym floor.

Was Danny entering the ABAs this year...? When were the Northeast

Divs and at what stage were we likely to meet if we both came through...? Before his fighter could answer, Tony Burns interjected:

"Worry about the Northwest first because, looking at you, you wouldn't win the Junior ABAs...."

I would later learn that it was simply his way to be parsimonious with compliments. Some young men couldn't handle being spoken to so brusquely and never went back to the gym, but I understood it from the off. Tony Burns was a psychologist and anyone who got to know him was eventually in receipt of a grizzled affection that was all the more precious for being hard won.

I made two subsequent trips to Bethnal Green before fight night. On the first occasion, I sparred with middleweight, Elliot Matthews, who didn't do much in the vest but went on to become English Champion as a pro. On the latter visit, Commonwealth Games Gold Medallist Darren Barker, floored me with a peach of a left uppercut that I didn't see. One might be tempted to ask how I know it was a left uppercut but it's not something I can explain. I'd been knocked down a few times in the gym over the years, but this was the only shot that ever truly short circuited my senses. I actually presumed It had been a slip until I got up and experienced a crackling sensation in my head. A quote I had read years before, attributed to Floyd Patterson, suddenly made sense.

"When you're knocked down with a good shot you don't feel pain. Maybe it's like taking dope. It's like floating. You feel you love everybody - like a hippie, I guess."

That's exactly how I felt but I didn't allow the incident to impact negatively on my confidence. Darren was a middleweight, in any case, and his future achievements confirmed that I didn't get knocked down by some second rater. It was another lesson learned.

My 34th birthday passed - necessarily- without traditional celebration. The layman tends to assume that an alcoholic must be a daily drinker, physically dependent on his poison, but that is frequently not the case. Although I didn't really have a problem abstaining from the booze in the run up to a fight, I would find myself constantly fantasising about getting pissed. A few days earlier I had attended Ed's birthday gathering in Kington and found it hard going, knocking back the Kaliber while everyone else got slaughtered. It occurred to me that if I won the Northwest Divs then the period of self-denial would have to be extended. Essentially, it was a conflict of interests.

That night, I stayed at Ed's place in Norbiton with a view to spending some quality time with my best mate ahead of the big day. To my chagrin, however, he left me in the flat and didn't return until the small hours due to his attempts to seduce a pair of young lesbians who lived around the corner. In fairness, both girls came to the fight so it could have been argued that he was out selling tickets on my behalf. If memory serves, he ended up nailing both of them in due course.

The next afternoon, we caught a train to Waterloo accompanied by a mutual friend called Johnny who was making a short documentary film about my unlikely comeback for a college project. From Waterloo we took the Jubilee Line to Wembley Park and made the ten-minute walk to Brent Town Hall where the battles would commence. We were amongst the first to arrive, several hours before the doors opened, and I was told that I couldn't weigh in because the Official In Charge was still en route. When said personage arrived half an hour later, I tipped the scales at 67.9 Kg, the lightest I had been in years. Every other boxer I knew was in the habit of not eating on the day of a fight until after the weigh in, but I didn't believe in that. As per my regular routine, I'd had yoghurt for breakfast and tuna with rice for lunch and still came in more than a kilo under the limit. I wasn't hungry but thought I had better grab a sandwich and a bottle of water from the nearby Morrison's in an effort to put on a bit of weight.

The worst thing about competitive boxing is the anticipation in those final hours before the first bell. The constant visualisation and repeated mantras juxtaposed with nagging doubts and sightings of potential opponents who look like King Kong and

Godzilla rolled into one. As Johnny rolled the camera, looking to capture anything of artistic merit for his 'fly on the wall' masterpiece, I mentioned that former World Light-Heavyweight Champion, Harold Johnson, had once likened boxing to 'walking in the cemetery at nighttime.' On the plus side I didn't feel as nervous as I had done in the smoke-filled working men's clubs as a kid. Those days had represented a whole different level of stomach-churning dread.

By degrees, the large municipal venue began to fill up with paying punters as my allies and supporters arrived and made themselves known. John Jacobs cut a splendid figure in his ABA blazer and enigmatically ceremonial chains although he nearly asphyxiated himself whilst negotiating the Town Hall steps. Duncan and Alfie converged on the scene with a bus load of Angel boxers clad in yellow and blue track suits just as the draw was being held to determine who would fight who in the name of Northwest London bragging rights.

There were 6 entrants in the Welterweight category:
Jamie and Jamal Morrison from All Stars who - being blood brothers - were presumably hoping they wouldn't be obliged to fight each other. Larry Ekundayo was also representing All Stars having switched clubs since our meeting last summer. That left George Hillyard from Kronk St. Pancras, Dermott Barrett from Trojan ABC and your truly. I didn't watch the random selection procedure, but it was soon relayed to me that I had drawn a bye to the semi - final and would fight the winner of Ekundayo vs Jamie Morrison. Jamal Morrison had also gotten a bye and would take on the winner of Hillyard vs Barrett.

The tournament got underway starting with the lighter weights and relevant results were fed back to me incrementally. Morrison beat Ekundayo which meant I would be fighting him. Hillyard beat Barrett but lost a disputed decision to the younger Morrison brother meaning that, if I should lose, then the siblings would meet each other in an historical final held over for the following week. I had never trained harder nor been fitter in my entire life and neither had I ever wanted something so badly. Various of my nearest and dearest were in the house and even the cute lesbians were present and correct. It was now or never.

I hadn't actually set eyes on my opponent until I saw him in the opposite corner. Mixed race with an Adonis build and huge biceps, it was a mystery how he made 69kg without resorting to amputation. Nonetheless, I was too long in the tooth to be intimidated by big muscles and won the first round handily, circling in both directions and picking him off with combinations whenever he invaded my personal space. Back in the corner, I turned to my throng and shouted, 'Easy way to make a living ...!" in shameless mimicry of my idol from Louisville.

The frivolity was knocked out of me in Round 2 when he landed a big right uppercut that caused my legs to do an involuntary dance as I attempted to avoid the two fisted follow up. When the ref stepped in and administered a standing count, I had no complaints this time around. I was 'buzzed', and blood was flowing freely from a cut that had opened underneath my chin. It was a strange place to get cut and the third man soon had occasion to halt the action again in order to get the doctor's opinion. Sensing that his man was about to be declared the winner by TKO, I heard one of the All-Stars Mob shout: "HE BLOWIN' IT, JAMIE... HE'S FELT THE POWER...!"

The doctor allowed the fight to continue and by the end of the round, I had weathered the storm. After a quiet third stanza in which neither one of us held the advantage, Alfie decided to try his hand at motivational speaking. Aware that I had dedicated the night to my late father, he began:

"BEN, DID YOU LOVE YOUR DAD...? 'COS YOU'VE GOT A FUNNY WAY OF SHOWING IT RIGHT NOW. YOU'RE BOXING LIKE A COMPLETE WANKER...!"

Although Duncan would later take issue with his approach, it had the desired effect as I produced a storming finish and won the 4th round by a street. At the final bell, my lot seemed to think I'd done enough but I had a bad feeling which was duly confirmed when the obligatory old, aged pensioner on the microphone announced, "AND THE RESULT OF THE SEMI FINAL AT WELTERWEIGHT... IS MORRISON IN THE RED CORNER...."

The dream had ended before it began and despite the torrent of backslappers insisting I had been robbed, I was forced to acknowledge the bottom line: I'd had 3 comeback fights to date and lost them all. With Johnny seeking a suitable denouement for his real life drama, I announced my 'retirement' and pledged to 'make the Angel kids great.' "It's been a blast but that's it for me," I concluded. As friends and well-wishers gave me a rousing ovation in the lobby, it suddenly occurred to me what a huge song and dance had been made for a horse that had fallen at the first fence.

Some years ago, Andy Blade had written a barbed couplet about precisely this aspect of my character that favoured hype over substance:

'Nothing special but such lofty claims
 You're goofing out instead of taking aim.'

Tonight, I had taken aim and missed. I could live with that. One day.

5/ JACKIE O

My 'retirement' was short lived after John Jacobs offered me a farewell fight on the Angel club show scheduled for March 25 at the Boston Arms in Tufnell Park. Like a luckless gambler who strikes out three times on red, I couldn't resist another spin of the wheel and was convinced that my luck had to change. On the night - a week shy of my official ABA birthday - I fought a kid from Battersea who answered to the name of Soldier Edo and dominated every round. As the MC announced "...AND THE WINNER OF BOUT NUMBER 10.... A UNANIMOUS DECISION, DOUGHTY IN THE RED CORNER..." I raised my arms and kissed my opponent on the cheek before sinking to my knees and kissing the canvas in papal style reverence for the sacred ground I had trodden for the last time. A little over the top perhaps but you are surely getting a feel for your narrator by now...?

As the formality of a raffle closed the show, it was all smiles in the downstairs dressing room as friends filed in and out with their congratulations and post-fight reviews. I changed into my grey Harlem thrift store suit and suggested we head to Camden Town in order to celebrate. There had been no ABA title and no Olympics but at least I had gone out a winner. There was actually no real reason for me to call it a day beyond the arbitrary ruling that a man of 34 was suddenly too old to get punched in the face for nothing. The lad I had bashed from pillar to post not 10 minutes earlier was 22. He ought to retire before I did, I was tempted to argue.

The entourage hit the Dublin Castle for around 90 minutes before spilling back onto the Parkway where we were suddenly accosted by a biracial rude boy duo. The white one of the two, who was about as menacing as a Harry Enfield caricature, made an obstruction of himself and enquired "Have you got any money for me...?" Assuming he was joking, I looked to indulge in some assertive banter before Kat lent her particular brand of charm to an inflammatory situation. I didn't hear what she said but the white one swore blind she had used the N - Word with reference to the black one and consequently tried to attack her. As I got in between he protested, "Look, I've got no problem with you, blood, but she is a racist bitch, y'now…!" It was the first time I'd heard the term 'blood' in a youth argot context on London streets, but it seemed to catch on like wildfire thereafter.

Within seconds, the ensuing scuffle came to the attention of a passing riot van, which resulted in two of its occupants disembarking to ask what all the fuss was about. Caucasian rude boy explained that he was attempting to chastise a racist whilst I argued there had been a misunderstanding based on phonetics. For good measure, I told them about my triumph at the Boston Arms, hence the reason for our peaceful celebration. The revelation appeared to see us home and dry as one of the officers smiled and said, "Yeah, I can tell from your nose that you box…!" The rude boys were told to get on their way and our party was allowed to continue its procession towards Camden Tube. After saying goodbye to everybody, I headed back to the Green Man with Carina, who was staying with me for a few days on one of her constant visits to the capital. Back in 'Bedsit Land' - consumed by an enormous sense of closure and fulfilment - I opened a bottle of whisky and so began another bender.

A certain type of alcoholic goes on a several days bender in a futile attempt to claw more of life's magic then he can possibly hold. Like a Kensington socialite maxing out Daddy's account until the bank refuses to honour the cheques, he emerges broken, remorseful and overdrawn. It is often thought that we drink to such damaging excess because we are intrinsically unhappy, and something is wrong in our lives. Remarkably, I didn't think there was anything wrong with my life and any suggestion that my organic self-esteem was dwarfed by a rampant, fragile ego would have been laughed out of court. I was never going to see the light so long as I had a roof over my head and money for the next drink but bear with me for the next 13 years and your patience will be rewarded.

Around this time, the work dried up at IFF causing me to seek employment in a call centre off Goswell Road at a company called Continental Research. If the regime at IFF had been reasonably laid back, then Continental was rather more draconian with its rules. Workers were assigned a booth for the day - which automatically stopped me from sitting next to the chick I found most aesthetically pleasing - and it wasn't uncommon to be verbally reprimanded for talking to the person next to you, Also, whilst the workforce at IFF consisted mostly of students and out of work actors, Continental boasted an altogether different demographic of young urban Londoner's who communicated with one another in the new 'Jafaican' patois that seemed to have engulfed the inner city. To make matters worse, I soon realised that my personal cachet with this crowd was practically non-existent as they tended to view any colleague in his mid-30s who hadn't risen to the rank of supervisor as something of a loner and a fuck up.

The miserable work environment not withstanding things were moving forward at the club, although Duncan and I were now at loggerheads on a constant basis. The battle lines were clearly drawn I insisted that his insight was minimal due to the fact that he'd never been in the ring whilst he argued that 'boxers make the worst coaches.' Had he done his homework he could have cited Ray Arcel, Cus D'Amato, Angelo Dundee and various other illustrious nonparticipants in support of his theory but I certainly wasn't going to tell him. The situation had become tense and potentially explosive but - as luck would have it - Duncan suddenly left under his own steam after falling out with John Jacobs, which was easily done, admittedly. He came to remove his gear from the gym one evening and I never saw him on the boxing scene again.

After Duncan's departure, former British title challenger turned trainer, Colin Lake, took over the senior coaching duties, assisted by fellow ex pro, Ivor 'The Engine' Jones. That left myself and a guy called Tommy - who had been a promising boxer in his own right before suffering from Crohn's Disease - to look after the junior sessions downstairs. From that moment forward, any thoughts I had of mentoring John Ryder evaporated as 'Lakey' took the teenager under his exclusive wing and painstakingly moulded him into a national novice champion and eventually a world class pro. In order that I could go in the corner with my boxers, I took the ABA Assistant Coaching badge which was hardly rocket science and chiefly involved keeping one's mouth shut. Lakey was the Guvnor upstairs and I was the main man on the ground floor. I suppose it was all about levels.

By late Summer, I was in several weeks' arrears at the Green Man and decided that leaving made more sense than paying. So, with Mr. Jacobs' blessing, I stored most of my belongings in the gym and went to stay at my mate Bealing's house in Kew Gardens until I was in a better position. Bealing was a troubled soul who still lived with his parents at the age of 26 but they didn't seem to mind me sleeping on the sofa for numerous nights in a row. I don't recall either of us formally asking their permission, I simply set up camp on a 'no news is good news' basis. After a few weeks, I had saved enough money to rent a studio in Finsbury Park although my tenure didn't last long. The rent was more expensive than it had been at the pub, so it seems curious in retrospect that I saw it as an expedient move.

During this period, Ed met a shy, alternative American chick with Azure blue hair and fell head over heels in love. She called herself Varrick - after a street in lower Manhattan - and following an accelerated courtship they married at Norbiton Registry Office, two weeks before Christmas 2004. Naturally, I felt a tad usurped in his priorities, but I refrained from taking an overdose the day after the nuptial ceremony unlike Simon who - being Ed's other regular sidekick- was apparently distraught. We remained very close but when a dame appears on the scene, no 'bromance' is ever quite the same. My mother had warned me that all 'wingmen' grew up and settled down eventually and strongly recommended that I do the same.

As soon as 2005 began, I bailed from Finsbury Park and put my things back in storage at the gym. On this occasion, I paid the landlord in full which felt so much better than disappearing like a thief in the night. Failing to pay debts and reneging on one's word simply builds up bad karma for a man and I would reap my fair share in the years that followed. Bealing and his dad helped me with the conveyance and - after packing my boxed possessions under the staircase at Angel ABC - we went to the Alma on Chapel Market for a beer. It was a Friday night and within minutes of our arrival, a disagreeable punter took an irrational dislike to Bealing and seemed hell bent on having a row. I tried to diffuse the situation with humour but when it became apparent that the coked up, drunken idiot wasn't going to leave my mate alone, I offered him outside.

Initially, my exit through the saloon doors became his excuse to chase poor Bealing around the pool table in the manner of a silent black and white comedy but when he stepped into the street, I hit him in the head with a straight right hand. A look of genuine shock replaced the arrogant sneer as he promptly retreated to the safety of the bar but, in hot pursuit, I landed another right hand that laid him out cold on the floor. I'm well aware that whenever a man relates an anecdote of fisticuffs it invariably ends with a stunning KO in his favour, but this fool really did go out like a light. Fearing that I might become another former boxer on a charge of involuntary manslaughter, we left our drinks and scurried down the road to the sanctuary of the gym. John Jacobs didn't approve of unauthorised visits, but I had the keys and this was an emergency. Deciding to stay put for the night, after stocking up with Kronenbourg, we slept on the canvas in the upstairs ring, although I struggled to nod off with the adrenaline coursing through my veins. I'm guessing my comatose adversary recovered since I never saw anything in the local news to suggest otherwise.

In need of another place to crash, the London Borough of Hounslow beckoned as the next stop on my relentlessly nomadic journey. Ed and Varrick had recently become friendly with an American guy called Josh who shared a house in the area with an old punk rock singer and invited me to come and stay for a month. Josh hailed from New Jersey but was one of those Anglophile yanks who preferred UK culture and the rarity value he was afforded within its confines. He saw himself as quite the bon vivant, with his 2-tone spiky hair, and seemed to have a few girls on the go at once. The pride of the collection in my estimation was a burlesque dancer from Detroit who went by the name of Jackie O, or 'Scarlette O' Harlette' when doing her turns. I was half smitten the moment I saw her and suspected it was mutual. Any impure thoughts ought to have been banished in the name of common decency, of course, but it just didn't play out that way. In my experience, it never does.

During my stay at Josh's, a few of us went out one night and chanced upon a pub on Essex Road called the Duke of Clarence. The landlord was a crazy Nigerian man who - apparently unacquainted with the basic commercial premise of his new venture - insisted on giving us unlimited free drinks all night. Before we arrived, the bar had been empty which seemed strange as it looked every inch a perfect spot for the North London bohemian set. Props included an old red phone box, some traffic lights and rock posters aplenty. Our host, who gave his name as 'Tayo', would continually bellow, "WELCOME TO MY BAR...!" before cackling maniacally and pouring more tipples for all and sundry. He claimed to be a property developer who had bought the pub as a pet project to let off some steam.

Letting off steam also included intermittent trips to the basement during which he left the bar unmanned and instructed us to help ourselves. On one occasion - mindful that I had a week's grace at the Hounslow pad - I ventured downstairs to find him seated in a leather chair, snoring a line of coke off a length of wooden board. "Do you want a line...?" he asked, his eyes still fixed on the skinny rows of white powder.

"Err... No thanks, Tayo. But I was wondering.... Do you happen to have any spare rooms here...?"

He looked up from his recreation and said, "Yes. Do you want it...?"

"How much are you asking for...?"

"£75 a week and I might need some help on the bar when we're busy."

It sounded good to me and so we shook hands on the deal before heading back upstairs. "BEN IS GOING TO BE MOVING IN...! CAN YOU IMAGINE...?" he cried to the assembled company before breaking into that trademark cackle.

As the coke became more prevalent, I made my excuses and left shortly after midnight, but Josh and Jackie stayed until sunrise on a bender that culminated in her dancing on the bar, or so he told me. Returning to the house at 10am the next morning, he saw fit to exclaim, "She's DANGEROUS...!" The tone was almost self-congratulatory, but he would be spared from her nocturnal ribaldry soon enough.

I moved into the Duke of Clarence the following week as Tayo quickly set about destroying any semblance of a viable business in favour of spawning a haven for drug dealers, fantasists and various strains of dangerous pond life. My designated room had clearly been occupied quite recently as it was littered with various items belonging to the previous tenant, including a blue acoustic guitar. I got the impression that whoever it was had left under a cloud since I also found some hospital paperwork relating to a serious head injury - apparently suffered by my unfortunate predecessor when he was attacked outside the pub with a blunt instrument. According to the notes, he had been found unconscious in the street and was unable to recall any details appertaining to his predicament. Although I was too egotistical for any admission of cold feet, I began to suspect that this next chapter would not be known for its tranquillity.

Tayo didn't appear to be affiliated with a brewery and when his existing stock ran out it was replenished with ad hoc trips to the local Costcutter. Outside, there was no name above the door which made me wonder if he had any legal entitlement to be there in the first place. In the first days of Spring, there were parties, gigs and happenings attended by the bright young things of EC1, but the vibes degenerated quickly and were marred by outbreaks of violence. In addition to being an unofficial bouncer, I was frequently asked to serenade the clientele with acoustic performances and the constant demands made me reluctant to pay rent.

One evening shortly after I took up residence, I got a text from Jackie saying that she wanted to come by and talk. When she arrived, it was obvious from her body language and demeanour that she was keen to progress our friendship to a more intimate status. Jackie had 99 problems and was looking for a knight in shining armour to take them all away. As she moved in for a clinch, I asked her, "What about, Josh.?"

"We talked tonight and agreed that we're not exclusive."

Rightly or wrongly, it was all I needed to hear by way of a green light as we began to begin to 'make out' in the otherwise empty bar. Empty except for Tayo who was on hand to provide the liquid fuel for our carnal desires. Perhaps hoping to see a live show, he suddenly produced 3 ecstasy tablets but I demurred leaving them to take 1 and a half each. Despite the general tendency of MDMA to make a person sensuous and fuzzy, Jackie became rather aggressive and duly revealed a penchant for biting and bondage on whatever he had fed to her. I woke up the next morning hungover but with that familiar sense of triumph that comes with another notch on the bedpost. I phoned the Continental hotline and told them not to expect me at work for the day.

Standing naked with her rear to me, Jackie O surveyed the detritus on my bedroom floor and wondered, "Where are my clothes...? Did I take 'em off up here...?" She had a swallow tattoo on her lower back and a shapely behind, albeit a tad on the slender side. I, too, was unsure where her garments had been discarded but - however you chose to dress it up- Josh would be proven right.

She was dangerous.

6/ YOU'VE BEEN FRAMED

Conditions at the Duke of Clarence made it basically unfit for human habitation, at least on a commercial basis. Hot water was erratic and the shower didn't work, making me grateful for the facilities at the gym. My fellow tenants were lost souls and fly by nights, although I did forge a good rapport with a scouser called Andy who gave me the lowdown regarding Tayo's backstory. He didn't own the pub but was unofficially leasing it from a dodgy band of Irish brothers with a local reputation and alleged connections to that most notorious of North London families. Tayo was a married man and father of one who had taken on the place in the hope it would be a vehicle for attracting as much extra curricular pussy as he could handle but he simply didn't have the discipline or financial savvy to keep the Irish mob off his back. One night, Andy had returned to find him tied to a chair and gagged whilst one of the brothers and his henchmen expressed their displeasure at his tardiness in paying the rent. Eventually, he convinced them to let him go but not before the point had been made. Andy was also refusing pay rent, arguing that he had saved the man's life. "You can't put a price on that," he reasoned.

Shortly after my card had been marked, I was heading downstairs to what passed for the kitchen one morning when I overheard an Irish accent shouting, "I SWEAR TO GOD, TAYO, IF THE MONEY'S NOT PAID, THERE'LL BE NUTTIN' A' THIS PLACE LEFT FOR YE...!" The author of the threat was a man in his early 30s with longish curly hair, clutching a cheap Nokia phone to his ear whilst reading the riot act. At the conclusion of the call, he offered his hand.

"Hi, my name's Barry. Do you live here...?"

"Alright mate...? I'm Ben. Listen, I couldn't help but overhear your conversation just then, Barry, and I got the gist of it. If he doesn't pay, how does that affect the rest of us...?"

"Oh, don't worry about that, mate. It's his problem not yours. Tell ye' what, I could murder a drink. Do ya' want one...?"

We went downstairs to the bar and he fixed us a couple of vodkas mixed with Ribena for want of anything else available. Sarcastically, he enquired, "Would you like ice…?" before expressing his general disdain at the sheer state of the place since Tayo had taken over. "No fuckin' idea how to run a business," he sighed. He wasn't a big man physically but evidently saw himself as a big player as he proceeded to tell me just how dangerous and connected he was.

"Have you noticed that bandage on his arm…?" he asked.

I had indeed noticed that Tayo wore an elasticated bandage on his right forearm but hadn't thought much of it.

"That was from the last time he was late with money. Tied him up for 40 hours and set him on fire."

I wasn't sure if I was supposed to be frightened or impressed but when he asked, "What's your game, Ben..?" I told him that I was a boxing coach. Suddenly he made to throw a punch with his left hand which I pretended to block.

"Ahhh.. You've still got it..!" he remarked like a man who got his dialogue from low budget gangster movies. I didn't know how much of his performance was a front and I didn't have time to find out. Tayo didn't live on the premises and arrived at noon most days but what he might do on this occasion was anybody's guess. Regardless, I was due at work in an hour so, bidding my new acquaintance farewell, I left via the side entrance and caught a 38 bus down the road.

When I returned at around 9.30pm, I found Tayo behind the bar unharmed and as manically ebullient as ever. I mentioned that an Irishman had been looking for him that morning, giving it the proverbial 'big one.' Shaking his head wistfully, he replied:

"Ben, we must NEVER succumb to bullies."

Despite his admirable maxim, people seemed to be getting hurt on a regular basis in an environment that was plain bad news. A guy called Kristian who lived upstairs and was pretty much a harmless geek was reportedly tied to a chair and had 3 ribs broken, although I had no idea what he'd done to deserve it. Then a young lady who also stayed on the premises suffered a broken jaw after arguing with one of Tayo's lackeys on a Saturday night. Both of them fled immediately afterwards in what was beginning to resemble a 'murder mystery' weekend with tenants dropping like flies. Our humble proprietor never seemed to get any sleep and consumed enough gear to approximate the Swiss alps, whilst the indie crowd and the girls had long since been replaced by 'ner do wells' from the surrounding rough estates. It was nothing but an illegal drinking den and I decided it was time to leave in search of greener pastures.

Jackie went back to Josh twice in the early days of our turbulent fling but I was so hopelessly besotted that I swallowed it and forgave her. He who ignores flagrant red flags in pursuit of a bewitching cunt shall always come a cropper, a wise man ought to have said. Jackie's life was full of drama. She was chasing fame and money and constantly talked about getting married so she could stay in the U.K. A romantic at heart, I went along with the projections of matrimony and moved into the small room she rented in a shared house in Shadwell. My habit of shacking up with a girl when I needed a place to stay was a recipe for unhappiness and even the good times were laced with comical misfortune.

One morning we woke up in a flat on Settles Street, rented by a friend of hers who was in Paris for a few days. He had given her the keys in order that she could take advantage of the Wi-Fi and get some work done while he was away. Despite a rocky start, we were in that honeymoon period when the sex is constant and undying love is copiously professed on both sides. As we lounged in bed exchanging sweet nothings, I suddenly asked,

"Are you hungry, baby...?"

"I'm starving," she replied. "You know what I really fancy....? Subway.....But I don't think there is one around here."

"If the lady desires Subway then she shall have Subway. Fear not, my darling...!" I declared whilst rising from the bed to get dressed.

"Baby, are you sure...? You're gonna' be gone for ages....! Do you have money..?"

"I've got my card,"

"No, take my purse..."

She handed me a decidedly effeminate red purse that I stuffed into the pocket of my black trousers before heading out the door towards Whitechapel High Street. Turning left in the direction of Aldgate, I kept my eyes peeled for a branch of the popular American sandwich chain. I'd gotten as far as Cornhill without any joy when I came to a fork in the road and was unsure which way to proceed. As I stood still for a moment and pondered my best direction, I suddenly became aware of two typically large City of London coppers staring at me with a modicum of suspicion. Reflexively, I returned their hostile gaze as they crossed the street and walked towards me. The bigger one of the two, who had a northern accent, did the talking:

"Excuse me, mate, can I ask what you're doing in the City today..? It's just that you look a bit suspect and you seemed very aware of our presence."

I told him that I was looking for a Subway outlet. "I've got a new American bird on the go and I'm trying to keep her sweet, know what I mean...?"

The bonhomie in my tone seemed to annoy him vaguely. "Well, everyone's got a great story but we get a lot of thieves in this area. Let's have a quick check of your pockets…"

Exasperated at such victimisation - having totally forgotten that I was carrying Jackie's purse - I went to turn out my pockets when they pushed me up against a wall and Northern Cop warned, "DON'T MAKE ANY SUDDEN MOVEMENTS..!" Instinctively, I clenched my right fist causing him to surmise, "Oh, and now you're getting aggressive… We'd better put the cuffs on. Done a bit of boxing, have ya'…? Well, you've picked the wrong people if you're looking for a fight today…"

After I was handcuffed ,he searched my pockets and duly found the fat red, girlish purse before exclaiming, "Oh Dear…! What's this…?"

"It's my girlfriend's purse. She gave it to me so I could buy her a fucking Subway sandwich..! I'll give you her full name, address and phone number. Call her now and she will tell you who I am."

Northern cop shook his head, "You might have just burgled 'er 'ouse, for all we know. We'll have to sort this out down at the station"

Resigning myself to the inevitability of getting nicked, I gave my name which he spoke into his walkie talkie before reading my rights. "YOU ARE UNDER ARREST ON SUSPICION OF THEFT. YOU DO NOT HAVE TO SAY ANYTHING BUT IT MAY HARM YOUR DEFENCE IF YOU DO NOT MENTION WHEN QUESTIONED SOMETHING WHICH YOU LATER RELY ON IN COURT. ANYTHING YOU DO SAY MAY BE GIVEN IN EVIDENCE."

Within minutes a meat wagon arrived and I was ferried the short distance to Bishopsgate Police Station. When Northern Cop relayed the details of my arrest to the desk sergeant, even I began to think I was guilty. It all sounded so cut and dried. I was put in a cell and decided to do a bit of groundwork to kill the time before my inevitable vindication. When Old Bill phoned Jackie on the number I had given, she confirmed every word of my story but - presumably feeling as if they hadn't wasted enough people's time as it was - it was decreed that she must come to the station to confirm my identity.

She arrived about 40 minutes later, looking rather disgruntled as if the whole sorry episode had been my fault. My property was returned - along with her purse - and we were heading for the exit when I suddenly turned and addressed my abductors:

"Fellas…. I don't suppose you could direct me to the nearest Subway, by any chance…?"

Humourless and ungracious in defeat, Northern Cop muttered, "I think the nearest one is at Devonshire Row." It occurred to me that an apology wouldn't have killed him under the circumstances. At that moment, the old man's immortal words came flooding back to me: "Never has there been a situation in my life in which The Law was involved that came out to my advantage…."

On all available evidence, I was forced to concur.

7/ PANIC ON THE STREETS OF LONDON

Jackie was in Dublin for a few days to get her passport stamped when the next pivotal moment in my life occurred. Walking along Brick Lane one Friday afternoon, I turned onto Cheshire Street and happened to see Tony Burns sitting on a wooden chair outside the junk shop that his cousin looked after on his behalf. Not certain that he would recognise me, I made eye contact and waited for a reaction. Surveying the street like a Cockney Buddha, his eyes glimmered as he nodded in my direction and asked, "How's it going…?"

"Not bad," I conceded. "I've retired but I'm coaching at the Angel."

"Well, I know that," he replied. "I asked you how it's going…?"

"To be honest, it's a bit slow. Sometimes I wish I was at a big established club. Know what I mean..?

"Come down the Repton. We'll give you a job."

"Really…?"

"We're open 7 days a week and you know where the gym is. Stick your head round the door one night and I'm sure we'll work something out."

I walked away from the exchange on cloud nine and didn't even care about Jackie and her capricious affections for at least fifteen minutes. Repton was the Manchester United of amateur clubs and I half imagined myself on the verge of initiation into some secret world of esoteric boxing wisdom. There had to be a formula behind their unparalleled success and all would soon be revealed, I fancied. It seems odd in retrospect but that's how I felt at the time.

Within a matter of days I had made the switch and already had a green and yellow tracksuit bearing the legendary name. Breaking it to John Jacobs was never was going to be easy and he took the news every bit as badly as I expected. One would have thought I was abandoning a woman after 40 years of marriage as opposed to simply moving to a bigger and better club in order to further my own coaching career. To the best of my knowledge, he took the resentment to his grave but I was never going to stay with an outfit that hosted 2 shows a year and had one decent boxer when such an offer was on the table.

Any notions I held of a magic system were quickly dispelled as I joined the Repton senior coaching team and was pretty much left to get on with it. The junior regime on Tuesday and Thursday nights was more of a tight ship, essentially governed by the head coach's mantra of 'GET ON YOUR BACK FOOT' but the older lads would arrive at different times in the evening and there seemed to be less cohesion. The Repton juniors all appeared to have the same sharp counterpunching style that produced a conveyor belt of champions but the seniors were a mixed bag, ranging from the superstars like Gary Barker and Ryan Pickard to the also rans. Alongside Burnsy, my other main confederate was a guy called Joe Lyons who did a lot of the spade work purely for love whilst avoiding the limelight and glory. Burnsy received plenty of both but remained an enigma. I soon realised that he wasn't a trainer in the traditional sense and was better described as a mentor and figurehead. He never held pads and seldom gave technical advice but had an aura like no man I had ever met before.

The season was winding down when I came on board but I got to work a few corners with the maestro before the summer break. After handing up to him on the first couple of occasions, we went to a show in Earlsfield with an Asian kid called Kamal Abdul and I was promoted to chief second for the evening. Kamal won on points against an Irish international and I was rather thrilled to see the report in Boxing News a week later that read:
'Burns was only handing up on this occasion, with No.1 in the corner being former Angel ABC welterweight, Ben Doughty.' I

wanted to be somebody in the fight game and seemed to be heading in the right direction, although my personal life remained a mess.

Before moving to the Bath House in 1975, Repton had been based at Bethnal Green Working Men's Club on Pollard Row. By 2005, the latter was an alternative music and cabaret venue at which Jackie did gigs with a popular burlesque troupe called 'Burly Q.' Due to my association with her, I landed a job behind the bar on event nights and working conditions pissed all over Continental's tedious bureaucracy, it had to be said. The Guvnor was a big affable East Ender called Steve who encouraged me to have a good drink during my shifts. Lamenting that he was currently on the dry due to doctor's orders he stressed that his unfortunate circumstances shouldn't stop me from getting stuck in whilst serving the trendy clientele. He didn't seem happy unless I had a pint on the go, with a short on the side, at all times and would constantly ask, "Have you got yourself a drink, Ben..?" It was almost as if he was drinking vicariously through me. The till was a very basic affair that simply opened and closed which would have made pilfering very easy but I wasn't tempted to top up my wages. The job basically consisted of getting drunk whilst watching a bunch of hot chicks take off their clothes with appropriately kitsch irony and stealing money on top of that would have invited a rancid karma.

As idyllic as the above may sound, my relationship with Jackie was volatile and doomed. I suspect we were both a tad narcissistic and competing for headline status whilst our mutual insolvency placed a further strain on the dynamic. I believed that I was madly in love but it was a very selfish, libidinous and possessive form of love, not to be confused with the groovy kind that Phil Collins sang about. On the morning of July 7, 2005, I concluded it was over and walked out of the door. My plan was to do a day's work at the call centre and then crash at a friend's house before returning at some point to collect my things but tragic events conspired against me.

I walked up the Commercial Road to Aldgate East tube station and found it surrounded by emergency services, with sirens blaring and commuters being turned away. The roads were cordoned off and a police officer advised me to go home and forget about going to work anywhere near the City. I didn't know what had gone down but it looked heavy so I turned around and headed back to the house on Ronald Street. At first, Jackie didn't believe there had been an incident and merely thought I was trying to milk some more pathos out of our demise but when she turned on the radio it emerged that suicide bombers had detonated their wares on 3 separate London Underground trains and a bus in Tavistock Square.

With nothing to do except hang around, I invested in a bottle of vodka and shared it with Jackie and her Brazilian housemate, Claudia, in the lounge. The afternoon effectively became a funeral service for our romance and I hated every second of it. Perhaps finding the air too heavy, at one point she disappeared upstairs to the bathroom. Electing to follow my muse 5 minutes later, I found her in the shower, combing her wet hair and complaining about the knots in it. I stepped into the tub fully clothed and offered my assistance. She didn't resist as I pulled the red comb through her soaked black tresses but objected when I attempted to place a hand on one of her breasts. "Uh – Uh...!" she grunted with a forbidding hand gesture.

Half pleading, I suggested, "One last time...?"

She shook her head sadly. "No, baby. It wouldn't be the same..."

At this point there seemed nothing else to say, so I went back downstairs and took a large slug of neat vodka. As soon as she was dressed and ready, Jackie walked out of the front door without a word and that was the end of that. I wanted to go after her but knew it would be a waste of time and energy if I did. Her mind was made up and the ship had sailed. Despite the brevity of our acquaintance, it would take me a long time to get over her.

For the next 3 weeks, I stayed at a house in Kington where Ed had recently resided before he and Varrick escaped to the more desirable district of Highgate Village. I asked Burnsy if he had any storage space and he replied, "What have you got..? I'll put it next to Ronnie and Reggie's stuff." I thought he was joking but it turned out that he had a large cage in his Bermondsey lock up containing the surviving effects of the notorious Kray Twins. Being only 7 years younger, he had grown up with them in Bethnal Green and remained a loyal friend and constant visitor throughout the years of their incarceration. Consequently, they left most of their worldly possessions to him, including suits, jewellery, Rolex watches, reams of prison correspondence and even love letters that Reg had penned to his tragic bride, Frances. When he helped me move my things out of Jackie's place, using one of the many lorries belonging to his removals firm, he really did put them next to the vat of Kray memorabilia. But whether it was a practical decision or simply appealed to his sense of theatre was hard to say.

Soon, I found a room to rent in a shared house on Christian Street, off Commercial Road. I didn't feel a connection with any of my Eastern European co tenants and positively disliked one of them as he seemed to complain about everything. I was pining for Jackie and a thousand things would remind me of her on a daily basis, right down to the underwear mannequins in the shop windows of the local wholesalers. As I went through the days feeling utterly wretched and forlorn, I imagined her to be living a fabulous life in her world of baroque, surrounded by wealthy suitors. I ached for a new love to come along and obliterate her memory but when a man is feeling sorry for himself, he gives out the wrong signals to womankind and it becomes a vicious circle.

I felt marginally better in October when Sugar Ray Leonard came to visit the Repton. Burnsy had first met Ray in 1976 during the Montreal Olympics and had found diversion playing 5 a side football against the future all time great and various other members of the U.S Boxing Team, including Leon and Michael Spinks. That had been almost 30 years ago and I wasn't sure if their paths had crossed since. It was a big day and seemingly everyone who had ever had a connection to the club was present and correct, wearing the yellow and green. When a white minibus pulled up on the forecourt outside it was initially thought to be Leonard and his entourage until out stepped 'Mad' Frankie Fraser with a handful of no marks in tow for one of his Gangland Tours. Being as the local press were on hand to record a momentous occasion, this represented a potential embarrassment causing Burnsy and Chairman, Dave Robinson, to politely request, "Quick as you can today please, Frank...!"

When the fistic icon arrived half an hour later, he carried with him an aura of unrivalled splendour in his black velour tracksuit and yellow baseball cap. He shook hands and posed for pictures with everyone and signed endless shorts, gloves and vests. He reminisced with Burnsy about episodes he probably didn't remember and gave a fleeting exhibition of his skipping skills. When my time came to be introduced, I clutched the hand that was proffered to me and declared:

"You are my ultimate ring hero.... Bar nobody but NOBODY....!"

With the deferential ambience of the true star, he almost seemed to blush as he replied, "Aww.. Thanks, man...!" His air of class and humility was almost incandescent. Despite the reputation for being a hard nosed prick in negotiations, there was no doubt in my mind that here stood one of the most likeable and talented human beings into whom God had ever put breath. It was time for me to stop moping over pussy loved and lost, I suddenly resolved. Greatness had inspired me to man

8/ MOTHER

Around the time of the Sugar Ray visit, a huge black heavyweight hopeful walked into the gym, having recently served a 5 year sentence for the armed robbery of a string of London brothels. Weighing around 19st, his physique looked chemically enhanced but Larry swore it was genetic and he simply came from a long line of mountainous hulks. Despite his background, he was nothing like the 'road man' stereotype and almost seemed too mild mannered to be a fighter. The fact that he was studying for a degree in pharmaceutical chemistry lent further contrast although it added to the suspicion that he knew his way around 'sports medicine.' He wasn't talented but he was dedicated and he could bang. Given that the heavyweight division is intrinsically less competitive than the more median categories, any such specimen is usually deemed worthy of attention.

When the National Novices came around in early 2006, Larry duly annihilated two opponents en route to the London title. After he blitzed the unfortunate Joe Kacz in 18 seconds of the final at York Hall, there was an audible buzz in the venue about the new super heavyweight destroyer from the famous Repton. That buzz was somewhat dampened when we ventured to Derby the following week and our man was soundly outpointed by a semi competent novice who looked more like a cruiserweight in stature. In part, Larry attributed his poor performance to Burnsy's demotivating sound bytes in the corner. For as long as anyone could remember, the old guru had employed a tough love approach during the 60 second intervals and would frequently cast aspersions on a boxer's efforts - or even his sexuality - if he thought the occasion demanded. Some fighters responded well to that kind of psychology but Larry clearly wasn't one of them. "I never want him in my corner again," insisted the disconsolate London Novices champion.

Whether Mr. Burns' caustic advice had contributed to the defeat or not, it was pretty much the story of Larry Olubamiwo's unpaid career that he either knocked his opponent out or lost on points if he failed to connect. Those who followed his subsequent story will know that he turned over in a blaze of publicity with Frank Maloney and was briefly regarded as a threat on the domestic scene before being blown away inside a round by Big Bad John McDermott. A subsequent ban for PED use saw him return as a journeyman, suddenly denuded of the ability to make a man blink - much less hit the deck - in his drug free incarnation. In later years, he became an actor which was probably a more appropriate vocation for a man who played the part of a good friend until push came to shove.

By now I was working for Tony's firm, T.D Burns, on a regular basis. In the Repton tracksuits bottoms that he wore like a second skin one could be forgiven for thinking him a man of modest means, driven solely by his passion. In actual fact he was the multi millionaire director of a successful company that counted some of the big hitters in The City among its long standing clients. The job mostly consisted of relocating corporate entities from one site to another and there was little doubt that Burnsy was the best Guvnor in the western world. The workforce met at 7.30am every morning outside his house on Bonner Street and the day's toil was usually done and dusted by lunchtime. We were always paid on a Friday in £50 notes but anyone who needed a midweek sub only had to ask. Manual labour has never been my forte and I was hardly the company's greatest asset but he looked after me all the same.

One morning he took me off a job in a new office complex on St. Mary's Axe and explained, "I'll pay you for the rest of the day but I want you to spar with this pop star down the gym." When we arrived, it turned out to be Bradley Mcintosh from S Club 7 who was getting ready to take on Jack Osbourne in a 3 round charity fight in aid of the BBC Sport Relief campaign. When the muscular rapper informed us that that a couple of Beeb cameramen would be filming the session, Burnsy pointed to me and warned, "Well, he's gonna' bash fuck out of you in a minute. That's not gonna' look very nice on the BBC, is it...?" In all fairness, he wasn't bad for a member of S Club 7 although, on the night, he lost a decision to Ozzy and Sharon's son who had more celebrity gravitas at the time. The episode was very much typical of the Repton experience of glamour, television exposure and celebrity endorsement. To this day, it remains the default location for any major British film with even the remotest theme of boxing or villainy.

When the summer came around, I moved into a 3 bedroom flat in the heavily Muslim enclave of Cannon Street Road with Jenny and Jon, signifying a reunion of the old guard. As Jon has not been heard of since the middle of Volume 2, I ought to detail that he underwent a predictably downward spiral after his release from prison and duly hit rock bottom at the turn of the millennium. At the nadir, he claimed to have been sleeping in a hole in the wall near Gloucester Cathedral and stealing charity collection boxes in order to finance a burgeoning crack habit before rebounding into the forgiving arms of the recovery community. After a successful stint in rehab, he worked in addiction services and observed 4 years of total sobriety before moderating with alcohol and recreational drugs thereafter. He never could drink to save his life, in any case.

What Jon had gained in maturity, he had lost in active follicles and was completely bald by now. In similar if less drastic vein, I had given up the ghost a couple of years earlier having decided that the short/long rock star coiffure no longer had the volume to be credibly sustained. Consequently, I borrowed some clippers and embraced the close cropped style once and for all. I found it liberating and concluded that hair was an overrated aspect of a man's appeal after the age of 35. The fact that people constantly cited a resemblance to Lock Stock heartthrob turned Hollywood action hero, Jason Statham, did nothing to undermine my self esteem.

Things were certainly looking up after the misery of 2005. I was living with my two best friends, had plenty of readies in my pocket and was a valued member of one of the greatest amateur boxing clubs in history. More importantly, I was over Jackie O and the residual spell she seemed to cast over me when we went our separate ways. I did see her one more time when our paths randomly crossed in a greasy spoon on Whitechapel High Street one Saturday morning. She was with a clean cut English guy that I presumed to be her husband since news had reached me of her finding a Sugar Daddy and getting hitched. I happened to be leaving as they were arriving and, strangely, decided to dial her number as I walked up Vallance Road although I have no idea what I was planning to say if she had answered.

It was my intention to apply for a professional trainer's license with the Board of Control after serving a sufficient apprenticeship in the amateurs. An apprenticeship that I hoped would be crowned by at least one Senior ABA Champion to whom I could lay partial claim. In 2006, Gary Barker and Ryan Pickard were Repton's top hopes to achieve such an honour at 64 and 75kg respectively. Pickard was a flashy boxer with a raft of natural talent and a big right hand but seemed distracted by other interests since wining a silver medal in the World Cadets back in 2003. His classic good looks and impressive physique had earned him a string of modelling assignments and - despite an article in the Evening Standard that touted him as a future Olympian - one got the impression he wasn't fully committed to the Noble Art.

Gary, for his part, was a southpaw genius - slicker than a Brazilian wax with more panache than Versace. Being the brother of Darren and son of former ABA champ, Terry, he came from good fighting stock and seemed to have a golden future ahead of him. On Burnsy's orders, I sparred him twice before the NE Divs and found it a profoundly frustrating experience on both occasions. It seemed nigh on impossible to nail Gary with a clean shot and he was ridiculously accurate with his own punches. Never before or since did I so struggle to solve the gloved conundrum in front of me. In case you are wondering, that is high praise indeed.

Both lads came through the Divs thus advancing to the London finals at Crystal Palace where they experienced mixed fortunes. Gary beat one Dani Davis of Fitzroy Lodge and Chris Evangelou from Haringey without dropping a round in the process. Ryan boxed well for 2 rounds before being flattened in the next stanza by Dale Youth hot shot, George Groves. A week later, Gary decisioned future domestic light welterweight contender, Adil Anwar, at the pre quarter finals in Barnsley to secure his place in the last 8, scheduled for Liverpool in mid November. In the glory days of yore, it was not uncommon for Repton to have several national finalists but, this time around, Gary was the last man standing.

On Monday the 13th of November, I was walking home from the gym when a friend called to invite me to what amounted to a leaving party for his wife, who had come to the end of her duty as a nurse at the Royal London Hospital. I'd had a heavy weekend and was disinclined to venture out on a cold dark night but, cajoled by the promise of hot young nurses in attendance, I soon relented. They were congregated in the Good Samaritan on Turner Street and, upon arrival, my attention was immediately drawn to a tall attractive black girl with a certain coquettish appeal. As the party moved on to a joint known as the 'Tiger Bar', she and I broke the ice and went to the juke box together in order to pick out some tunes. Her name was Diana and she was clearly the product of a straight background - quite at variance with mine - but I liked her regardless and it seemed to be mutual.

At closing time, those who didn't have to work the next day jumped into a taxi bound for 'Mother Bar' in Shoreditch where our flirtation was consummated with a kiss at the bar. The choice of venue would prove extremely prophetic as we partied into the small hours before going back to my place in Shadwell. I awoke the following morning full of nature's amphetamines and took my new lady friend for a fry up at a local caff. Scoring on a Monday night seemed like a result and as I caught the train to Liverpool that afternoon, I merely hoped that young Gary Barker would continue the run of good fortune.

I checked in at the Adelphi Hotel in the city centre and found Burnsy, Gary and various members of the Barker family already in residence. The mood was confident despite the fact we had drawn the more experienced and highly fancied Bradley Saunders of South Durham ABC. Also in the mix was big punching Jamie Cox from Swindon but Gary was capable of beating anyone on his day, it seemed. Although our confidence was valid, it wasn't vindicated on the Wednesday afternoon when Gary went down 17-7 to an opponent who was that little bit too mature for him, despite being merely a year older. Inevitably, there was disappointment but the reassuring maxim that states 'There's always next year' seemed perfectly applicable without the benefit of hindsight.

A month later, Gary came along for the club's annual trip to Edinburgh although he only boxed an exhibition since the Gilmerton Club had no light welterweights of sufficient pedigree to match him. After the show, most of our contingent hit the town for a sojourn on which I distinctly remember Gary demonstrating a new way of drinking Sambuca that involved turning the empty glass upside down and snorting the fumes through a straw. The retrospective thought that he had little more than 24 hours remaining of his fabulous young life is a chilling one.

Feeling more drunk than usual, I elected to get a cab back to the hotel around at 1.30am and left the boys to it. The next morning I got up for breakfast and realised that Gary and another boxer called Ricky Beasley were only just returning from the night's revelry having not slept a wink. Unfortunately, upon returning to London, Gary invested too much faith in his youthful stamina and attended a professional show in Chigwell before making the tragic decision to drive up to Leicester in order to see his girlfriend - despite not having been to bed in 48 hours. Just before 6am on Sunday December 10, fatigue took its toll as he passed out at the wheel of his Ford Fiesta causing a fatal collision with the barriers on the M1 near Dunstable. He was taken to the nearest Hospital but died shortly afterwards.

It was a terrible waste of a fine young man that sent shockwaves through the British boxing fraternity but let his name be etched in immortality as the classy, mercurial southpaw that I (for one) couldn't catch with a handful of sand.

9/ BABY LOVE

Diana and I were dating but had called things off at least twice before discovering – in April 2007 – that she was pregnant. Her substantial reservations about my suitability as a father or a partner notwithstanding, I was enormously excited at the prospect of becoming a Dad. Rightly or wrongly I was also enamoured with the imminence of a mixed race baby as opposed to a standard Anglo Saxon offspring. As childish as it may sound, I figured there was a better chance of siring the next Sugar Ray Leonard if he had some Afro – Caribbean blood coursing through his veins. In my naivety, I couldn't see a downside to the situation but I would soon receive a crash course in the pitfalls of unplanned pregnancy in a merger of incompatible souls.

Coinciding with the accuracy of my seed was Jon's radical decline into a frighteningly accurate facsimile of his former self – the love sick psychopath. Whilst working at the Turning Point Project in Soho, he had forged a dalliance with one of the girls in the office, a delectable specimen who went by the name of 'George.' Initially, things went well but after the heady, romantic period of wooing, he began to exhibit the more disquieting aspects of his personality that were rooted in maternal rejection. George, whose misgivings began to mount during an especially fractious trip to Thailand, opted to tiptoe out of the relationship upon their return and left no forwarding address. Subsequently, Jon lost his mind and became obsessed with finding her. He began to keep strange hours and was no longer the cordial presence he had been in the household previously. In apparent homage to Columbo, he soon ascertained that she was living with friends in Canada Water and spent much of the next several weeks covertly tailing her, although what he hoped to achieve was unclear.

Just as he appeared to be emerging from the emotional crisis, he got a call from work one morning and awkward words such as 'Police', 'stalking' and 'hate crime' were suddenly bandied around. Evidently George had reported him for harassment and his presence was urgently requested at Southwark Police Station to explain his unhealthy interest in her movements. Upon arrival, he was banged up for several hours and grilled before being bailed to return several weeks hence whilst the Crown Prosecution Service deliberated. His phone was seized for the purpose of the investigation, which seemed to add weight to the gravity of his predicament.

That said, although the authorities took stalking claims more seriously in the 21st century, it seemed unlikely that he was looking at a 10 stretch in Parkhurst. Apparently incapable of weighing up the situation sensibly, Jon opted to flee to India – just in case. We were having a drink in the ironically named George Tavern on the corner of Jubilee Street one night when he suddenly pushed a piece of paper across the table that turned out to be a flight itinerary for New Delhi. It was his way of telling me that Jenny and I would need to find a new occupant for his room, unless we were inclined to make up the increased rental demand between us.

Unwilling to bring a stranger into the Cannon Street dynamic, we ultimately decided to bail and so I moved in with Diana when our notice expired. I told myself that it made perfect sense with a baby on the way but retaining my independence would have been the manlier thing to do in hindsight. Despite being 3 years shy of my 40th birthday, I was steadfastly reluctant to grow up and life suddenly seemed desperately unromantic, traipsing around Mothercare looking at cots and baby clothes. If anyone had a right to feel aggrieved it was Diana, who was 11 years my junior and didn't ask to be knocked up in the first place. Like me, she enjoyed a drink and could have used a bit of moral support during the 9 months of enforced sobriety but I was far too selfish and emotionally dependent on the booze to be capable of such an altruistic gesture. I did at least try to hide my consumption in the midweek but the spatial restrictions of a one bedroom flat in Forest Gate conspired against me. It wasn't as if I could quietly sip gin and tonics in the west wing.

With fatherhood on the horizon, I began to think about my long term career prospects above and beyond lugging office furniture for T.D Burns. Accordingly, my attention was drawn to an advert in Boxing News seeking trainers to deliver boxing sessions in schools across South London and Kent. The initiative – imaginatively titled Boxing 4 Schools – was the brainchild of former heavyweight contender, Wayne Llewelyn, and presented an opportunity to get paid for something I had done hitherto purely for love and prestige. After a couple of phone calls and a routine interview, I joined the team which included former British heavyweight champ, Julius Francis, and decent ex – pro, Harry Senior. For much of the time, I was paired up with Julius or Harry which suited me fine since Wayne and I never established an affable rapport. I just found him to be rather charmless and arrogant although it's entirely plausible that he felt the same way about me. He would constantly bang on about the need for 'lesson plans' and seemed obsessed with teaching Mayweather-esque pad routines to raw novices who scarcely knew one hand from the other.

Although it was fun showing feisty schoolgirls how to throw a right cross whist extolling the virtues of discipline to potentially wayward lads, wages were often late and Wayne would frequently criticise the manner in which we delivered the classes. The fact that I was unwilling to give up my position at Repton in favour of a total commitment to the project became a further point of friction. It was during a Sunday afternoon session at The George that I impulsively decided to quit the job with a cursory text, which annoyed Diana since I had no contingency in place. As ever, my attitude was that something would turn up.

As luck would have it, something did turn up – in the shape of another advert in Boxing News. An outfit called CityBoxer were looking for trainers to look after their wealthy client base at the Ring Boxing Club on Ewer Street near Southwark Tube Station. It seemed worth a try and so I rolled up at the gym in late August for an interview with a rather imposing lump of a man known as 'Burf.' I should probably clarify that he was somewhat over his ideal weight but had the stamp and bearing of a man who used to be in shape and had failed to adjust his ego accordingly. Right away, I saw him as a charlatan and not a person who was coming from an authentic boxing background. Like Duncan, he attempted to bamboozle real boxing people with a blizzard of opaque sports science terms and modern nutritional guff. 'Nutritionist heal thyself' sprang to mind as he waxed lyrical about macronutrients and energy systems – seemingly oblivious to his incongruously sizeable girth.

I outlined my experience as a boxer and coach and – perhaps unwisely – my general plans for world domination. Like some TV talent show despot, he suggested, "Ok Ben. How about you come down and have a workout next week…? We'll see how you box and take it from there." Although he wouldn't have lasted 5 minutes down at The Repton, he was the king of this enclave under a railway arch, built on male camaraderie and middle class testosterone. The message was clear that anyone who desired to join the vanguard would have to jump through hoops and dance to his tune.

When I returned for my 'audition' the following Tuesday, he didn't even deign to hang around, claiming to have double booked on a night that included family obligations. "Spencer will look after you, " he told me before disappearing out of the door with a woman and child in tow. 'Spencer' turned out be Spencer Fearon, a former light middleweight prospect with the looks and charisma to have made a big splash but apparently not the fortitude to match his undeniable talent. After his third unsuccessful challenge for Southern Area laurels, 'The Spirit' had retired to become a self styled guru and Britain's youngest black promoter, as he was fond of telling all and sundry. Like a schizoid amalgamation of Muhammad Ali and Arthur Daley made in

Kennington, he was a beguiling figure and we got on like a house on fire from that day forward.

Aware that the fat man sought an evaluation of my boxing skills, Spencer had me spar with a couple of the city boys plus a young amateur light welterweight by the name of Phillip Bowes. He turned out to be a future champion and everyone in the gym stopped to watch as we went back and forth for 3 rounds. "How old are you…?" asked Spencer when the session concluded.

"37.." I replied.

"You've got some black in you…!" he decreed approvingly.

Being afforded honorary black status was something I enjoyed in boxing circles and I hoped he would relay those sentiments to our absent friend whom he often referred to as 'the fat controller.' I took the gloves off and got busy doing a bit of pad work with some of the members, having broken the ice and shown my mettle as requested. Spencer, who could see genuine boxing acumen from a mile away, was impressed and assured me, "Don't worry. You'll be joining us very soon." Before I left, we talked a little about boxing history which further served to consolidate our instant kinship.

I got the job at CityBoxer although Burf dragged out my period of internship in order to assert his authority as the man who giveth and taketh away. Egos aside, I had to hand it to him; the brand he had created was the perfect embodiment of the white collar boxing concept. Corporate types knocking lumps out of each other within their mutual limits of semi competence with glitz and glamour superimposed. Alan Lacy had been the first on this side of the Atlantic to capitalise on a gap in the market for a gentlemen's league of 'blood and thumps' but CityBoxer did it better. The gym was a 'Boy's Own' environment in which dreams were sold – or more specifically rented – at premium rates. And I was quite prepared to suffer a clash of personalities for the lucrative pickings on offer.

Our first born son was predicted to arrive on Christmas Day but – as much as the prognosis appealed to my messianic delusions – fate had other ideas. On the evening of Sunday, September 9, Diana's waters broke dramatically whilst we were engaged in a vertical act of intimacy in the front room. Coincidence though it almost certainly was, I had a hard time convincing myself that the natural process hadn't been disturbed by our meddling but there was no time for recriminations or analysis. I phoned an ambulance which transported us to Newham Hospital in the dead of night whilst I informed our respective mothers of the unexpected development. I knew next to nothing about premature births and had certainly never heard of a healthy baby born at 6 months gestation. Jostling amongst the fear and uncertainty was a twinge of excitement that my wait to become a father was almost over. Perhaps it was all going to be ok.

For the first hour, nobody told us anything and the African nurse assigned to look after Diana was spectacularly sullen and unhelpful. Thankfully, a lady doctor eventually arrived on the scene with a far more palatable beside manner and softly explained, "It looks as if baby is going to arrive in the next 24 hours." I had no idea what that might mean in practical terms and, sensing my ignorance, her colleague asked:

"What do you know about babies born at this period of gestation...?"

"Not a lot but I'm guessing it's hardly ideal...?"

"There's going to be lots of problems," he said gravely.

If men were acclaimed for the veracity of what came out of their mouths then this guy would have had his lips bronzed. There would be an abundance of problems of a very real and taxing nature for the next 6 months and beyond. In perfect contrast, Jon turned out to be running from imaginary problems as the boys in blue confirmed there would be no charges brought against him, shortly before he flew to New Delhi. It seemed like a classic case of throwing out the baby with the bath water.

10/ SAVE A PRAYER

Joseph Cassius Doughty was born at 10.05am on Tuesday, September 11 in the University College Hospital, Fitzrovia. The previous day, Diana had been transferred from Newham to the Elizabeth Garrett Anderson Wing located behind Tottenham Court Road because it had vastly superior facilities for keeping radically premature babies alive. Joseph entered this mortal coil weighing scarcely 900 grams but seemed to have an implausibly strong grip as he clutched my index finger during our initial introduction. He looked impossibly tiny but had already made attempts to breathe under his own steam when plucked from the emergency slash in Diana's stomach. Seeking to maintain a brave visage for the doctors and nurses, I cried internal tears and screamed, "COME ON, SON...!" within the privacy of my head as I sought to summon every other – worldly power of religious folklore to assistance. Seeing through the facade, a female nurse asked if I was ok but I didn't quite know how to answer. It was the strangest concoction of emotions and I did feel rather robbed of the unmitigated tears of joy that every other first time father seems to describe.

Diana was home within days but Joseph would remain in the neonatal unit for several months with a 50 percent chance of survival at the outset. Life became a constant vigil of daily visits to check on his progress or lack thereof, depending on the rub of the green. A sudden drop in his 'sats' was cause for alarm and he was subject to more weigh ins than Harry Greb but, steadily, he grew into an increasing semblance of a normal child obscured by the skull cap and all manner of tubes and wires. Parents on the ward had a natural affinity and throughout this whole period, some babies went home whilst other poor mites perished. The contrasting fortunes of our confederates caused a polarity of emotion; I was a little envious of those for whom the ordeal was over but whenever news came of another baby who didn't make it, I thanked a nameless God for our relative good fortune. Against the backdrop of stress and strain, I continued to drink heavily, which did nothing to promote harmony in my domestic affairs. Diana and I argued constantly as our bubbling insecurities exploded on a regular basis.

On the plus side, I was knee deep in clients at CityBoxer and making a good wage. Burf's obsessive need to be the king of the castle was a constant source of annoyance but we got on superficially and I was excited by the potential of what might be achieved in cahoots. Spencer had recently been granted his promoter's license by the British Boxing Board of Control and was heading up an arm of the company called 'CityBoxer Pro.' To spearhead this bold assault on the disingenuous world of professional boxing, two young hopefuls had been signed in the shape of Jack Morris, a good looking light heavyweight from Margate, and an African light welterweight called Giovanni Kopoto. Both lads were employed in the gym in order to supplement the non existent income of a budding professional boxer at grass roots.

Turning pro might sound glamorous but the harsh reality for any ambitious fighter with pretensions of hitting the big time is that he will need to sell a minimum of 100 tickets every time he steps into the ring. Olympic medallists and sons of legends will have an easier commercial path but the average aspirational 'nobody' is basically paying his early opponents to lose to him in order to build some momentum. Unlike most of their ilk, Jack and Giovanni could count on a ready made fanbase of champagne swilling traders with large disposable incomes and a loyalty forged by regular acquaintance. It was an enviable set up, so long as they could actually fight.

The first and only Fearon/ Cityboxer promotion was staged on a Tuesday night in October at the Tower Bridge Hotel and didn't go according to the script. The formal dinner show was billed as 'Tear Up At The Tower' but 'Night Of The Underdogs' might have been a more fitting tag line as both house fighters went home with a loss. Giovanni was flattened in the second round by Sheffield trial horse, Daniel Thorpe, who seemed genuinely apologetic and shocked at his own strength. Morris gave a better account of himself but lost a razor thin decision to tough Polish journeyman, Michael Banbula, which garnered an angry response from special guest, Steve Collins. "HOW can you do that to a kid on his pro debut...?" demanded the former WBO champion of referee Ken Curtis, who was perhaps labouring under the misapprehension that this was a sporting occasion. It was likely that Banbula shared his frustration since winning in the away corner is bad for business.

In contrast to the general ambience of dampened morale, Spencer was visibly buzzing. The show had been a triumph, he insisted, and would serve as his blueprint ongoing in a jaded subculture that badly needed a shake up. "I'm not gonna' carry these bums if they can't fight," he proclaimed, milking every last drop of adulation and kudos in the room. His association with the fat man would be short lived but the meteoric rise would continue.

One afternoon in November, we paid our daily visit to the neonatal unit only to find that Joseph's incubator was conspicuously absent from its regular place on the ward. This caused a gut wrenching panic as we asked the nurse on duty what had happened to our baby. Solemnly, we were ushered into an office at the end of the corridor and informed of the bad news. As if he didn't have enough problems, Joseph had contracted a condition known as necrotising enterocolitis that was threatening to destroy his minuscule bowel as we spoke. He wasn't in a stable enough condition to be moved, they explained, but if we didn't take a gamble and get him to Great Ormond Street for emergency surgery as soon as possible then he was going to die anyway. There was no guarantee that he would survive the journey, never mind the operation.

In a collective and nightmarish daze, we made the nine minute taxi ride to the famous children's hospital, not daring to speak beyond standard pleasantries. Upon arrival we were told that Joseph had arrested in the lift and projections were very bleak. An Asian doctor warned, "You must prepare yourselves for the worst," while his female colleague decreed, "I'll let you have a couple of minutes with him but it's really not looking good." My instinct was to reply, 'I don't WANT a couple of minutes if he's not coming back...!' but I saved my breath for Joseph Cassius:

"You're not going ANYWHERE, champ...!" I whispered to the comatose little form in the incubator as it was rushed with great haste into another elevator, surrounded by a sea of green scrubs.

They didn't say how long the operation would take and I don't recall asking. Regardless, we had some time to kill and decided to go to a nearby pub for a meal, of all things. I suspect it was the alcohol that chiefly appealed to us both but – against my expectations – I managed to plough through a cheeseburger and chips without undue difficulty. Given that I had been sufficiently heartbroken on various occasions to render digestion impossible - purely down to the whims of some badly wired strumpet – I briefly questioned my sense of emotional priority. Throughout the ritual of dining, neither one of us alluded to the unspeakably awful situation that fate had inexplicably cast upon us. I dared not even think about it.

About an hour later, we returned to the hospital just in time to see Joseph being wheeled out of surgery looking ludicrously buoyant compared with the state in which he had entered. "Is that HIM...?" wondered Diana as if witnessing a paediatric version of the Resurrection . The medical professionals were smiling and happy to admit that their pessimism might have been a tad misplaced. "He has responded much better than we expected," said the lady doctor who had given us the last rites vibe less than 90 minutes ago. I had given the middle name of Cassius because it was the most powerful symbol for triumph over adversity that I could think of and – despite Diana's predictable objections – I was beginning to feel vindicated.

Soon we were seated in an office with a wonderful Irish gentleman by the name of Doctor Kylie who had performed the miracle. "I did Joseph's operation just now," he explained. "In simple terms, I removed the segment of dead bowel and the good news is that there is still plenty of healthy bowel left. The question is: is he strong enough to bounce back from this…? And the answer is we don't know at this stage but the indications are good."

Diana and I were given parental accommodation on site for the next 10 days while our child was closely monitored around the clock. Our temporary digs amounted to a charming holiday home in the metropolis and led to the indulgence of a fantasy on my part that I was in a sufficiently exclusive tax bracket to call it my own. During our short stay, I read the Jack Johnson biography 'Unforgivable Blackness' and after spending several hours with Joseph we would go to a nearby wine bar every night in order to down copious bottles of rosé. Since I preferred red and she favoured white it was perhaps the only compromise we were capable of.

Joseph wouldn't be home for Christmas but it wasn't long before he was back at the UCLH where he reached full term and suddenly resembled a regular baby. The saga continued to be a gruelling one with no imminent closure but at least the state of emergency seemed to be over. To mark the Yuletide season, CityBoxer management hosted a dinner party on the premises during which I learned that Spencer had effectively been fired. I neither knew nor cared about the particular reason for his dismissal but suspected that Burf's intolerance of another alpha male in the vicinity had a lot to do with it. In any event, Spencer didn't lose any sleep as he ventured across the river and set up camp at Alan Lacey's 'Real Fight Club' near Liverpool Street Station.

Joseph finally came home on St. Patrick's Day, 2008 although he remained attached to a portable cylinder of oxygen and required a plethora of medicines to be administered night and day. By now, Diana and I had moved out of the flat in Forest Gate and into her Mum's house in Plaistow where we intended to save for a new place with 2 bedrooms. I had amassed too many clients to justify staying on at Repton full time but still kept a foot in the door by virtue of showing my face in Bethnal Green every Wednesday evening. I enjoyed the status of being a Repton trainer but had been toying with the idea of quitting the amateurs and applying for my pro license for the past several months. It seemed absurd that coaches were obliged to make a choice between the two codes since there was no real reason why they couldn't happily co-exist but logic and bureaucracy have never been staunch bedfellows. Rightly or wrongly, the ABA regarded professional boxing and its participants as a cancer to the purity of sportsmanship and fair play. As the summer approached, my decision was precipitated by a modest proposal from Jack Morris.

"Might need you to train me for my next fight, Ben," he suddenly announced one morning during a moment of mutual downtime at the gym. We had done a bit of sparring in recent months and built the kind of rapport that would have made it difficult for me to refuse even if I'd wanted to. Although he was heavily under the influence of the fat man, I liked him a lot and was more than a little excited at the prospect of 'turning over.' He was never going to be a world beater but had solid foundations and carried a bit of a dig in his right hand. Being a good looking white boy with a corporate following he was also more commercially viable than an ethnic street kid with endless talent and half a dozen fans. We shook hands on the deal and I appeared before the Board on the first Thursday in June.

Sitting before the Southern Area Council in want of a trainer/second's license is somewhat akin to starring on the reality TV show, 'Dragon's Den.' The British Boxing Board of Control is a self appointed autocracy that trades very much on the historical prestige of its name, having formed in 1929 from the remnants of the Pelican Club in Covent Garden. For decades, the private limited company had ruled the UK fight game unchallenged and

Frank Warren's audacious promotion of a huge domestic clash under Luxembourg sanctioning was still 4 years away. In recent times, the bar seems to have lowered but in 2008, strangers and newcomers were treated with an entry level of suspicion and disdain.

As I was summoned to the oak panelled room above the George public house on Borough High Street on the afternoon in question, roughly 10 middle aged men in suits were seated around the table for the purpose of a ritual grilling. I figured that the Repton connection would stand me in good stead but was wary of revealing any association with the CityBoxer brand, knowing that the Board saw white collar boxing as only marginally more desirable than leprosy. The tone of questioning was uncongenial but not overly challenging to any person with a credible boxing background who understood that you don't put a fighter in the sauna on the day of a fight. I was briefly dismissed from the room before being recalled to hear the good news from former Southern Area Lightweight Champion, Phil Lundgren:

"Ok Ben, we're going to recommend your license. You can pay by phoning head office in Cardiff and you should get your laminate within a fortnight."

Like most novice trainers, I felt as if I had achieved something beyond the reach of mere mortals and hurried back to the gym like a conquering hero. Given that Burf's Hell's Angel business partner had already been knocked back twice for a promoter's license, I was more than happy to imply that only real boxing people were admitted to the inner sanctum. Little did I realise at the time that professional boxing on the bottom rung can be soul destroyingly dull and scripted.

Since losing his debut, Jack had gotten a points win over one Ricky Strike from Rotherham who – according to the minimal report in Boxing News – was inappropriately named as he scarcely threw a punch. A cursory search on boxrec reveals that

Strike didn't win any of his fights prior to retiring that same year but the better journeymen would often rack up triple figures, doing just enough to lose against all but the most inept of 'prospects.' As Jack '13' Morris prepared for Fight No.3, I gave it my best shot but it wasn't long before the fat man and I were at loggerheads over everything from the silly numerical nickname to the finer points of strength and conditioning. I could live with the constant references to 'VO2 Max' and the crucial importance of the 'condyloid joint' but when he vetoed a sparring session at TKO Gym in Canning Town purely because he wasn't invited, I began to lose my appetite for the job. After one disagreement too many, I made it clear that I would see Jack through his next public engagement scheduled for October and then I was done.

On the night in question at the Café Royal in Piccadilly, we won a 4 round decision over a guy called Sabiie Montieth who was making his debut and had taken the fight on less than 24 hours notice. He arrived wearing a tuxedo, apparently because he was employed as a bouncer at some upscale Central London establishment and had come straight from work. In fairness, he had also come to win and arguably did more damage than he incurred as Jack broke his right hand in the second round when connecting with his opponent's obstinate skull. For that, I was obliged to accept a portion of the blame since I had forgotten to bring the requisite gauze and adhesive tape that separates the amateur from the pro. Recuperating from such an injury, Jack didn't fight again for another 5 months by which time I was long gone.

Perhaps the fat man had been right about those condyloid joints after all.

11/ HARD KNOCKS FOR LIFE

Alan Lacey was a ducker and diver but had also been known to jump out of windows when the occasion demanded. Prior to his trailblazing of the white collar boxing phenomenon in the UK he had flirted with the pro game before a farcical night at the Brixton Academy in the summer of 1993 put paid to any such pretensions. On paper it was a good looking bill, featuring such luminaries as John Mugabi, Kirkland Laing and Gary Stretch but the event was plagued by various logistical problems, not least when it came to the exchequer. Upon realising that the coffers were insufficient to pay the vast majority of fighters and officials, our hero is rumoured to have faked a heart attack before escaping through a window in the gents toilets. Whatever the truth, it signified the end of Alan's promotional aspirations in the bigger world of boxing until he stumbled upon a bold new concept.

Having taken up recreational boxing in his mid 40s, Alan was intrigued by the inclusive culture that Bruce Sillverglade had reportedly created in New York where stockbrokers and lawyers trained alongside champions and contenders at Gleason's Gym. Considering it worthy of investigation, he flew across the pond and fought a Manhattan dentist over 3 rounds before returning to London at the turn of millennium with the germ of an idea. 'The Real Fight Club' staged Britain's first ever definitive white collar boxing shows and operated out of numerous makeshift homes until a gym was established on the corner of Curtain Road in 2007. I left Cityboxer a week after Jack's fight and rolled up at the premises in mid October looking for a space in which to ply my trade.

In terms of street credibility, there was no comparison between the two entities. Every Real Fight Club coach had a legitimate boxing resume, most notably Robert McCracken who trained his star pupil Carl Froch in house alongside a stable of lesser lights including Lenny Daws and Matthew Thirlwall. Spencer had reinvented his brand under the banner of 'Hard Knocks Promotions' and commandeered the office on the top floor as his base of operations. Reading between the lines, he had secured substantial corporate sponsorship via a handful of well connected traders who had been rampantly schmoozed in that inimitable way. The only major drawback was that it seemed 10 times harder to make a good wage in this new environment. Cityboxer had plied me with a constant conveyor belt of new clients but at the Real Fight Club there was very much an ethos of every man for himself. Trainers were obliged to pay a weekly ground rent and the management didn't particularly care if we made money or not, beyond that minimum requirement. I was too proud to admit that I might have been better off with the fat man, despite increasing pecuniary demands.

By the beginning of 2009, Diana and I had moved to a 2 bedroomed house in Stratford where we duly discovered that she was pregnant for the second time. After the flagrant ordeal of the first pregnancy and childbirth experience, I was rather grateful for a second crack of the whip. This time around her 'incompetent cervix' would be vigilantly monitored which would hopefully ensure the delivery of a full term baby who weighed more than a bag of cola cubes. The thought of another 6 month cotside vigil or worse was not an appealing one. Aside from that, I had a new pugilistic 'baby' with whom I nurtured hopes of breaking down the door to the big time.

The previous November, I had gone to the York Hall to support Larry Olubamiwo in his second pro outing and found myself smitten with a flashy Moroccan menace by the name of Yassine El Maachi. Sporting a deceptive 50/50 log going in, 'The Showman' resembled a bigger version of Naseem Hamed as he destroyed the previously undefeated Kevin Concepcion inside 2 rounds. Promoter Frank Maloney didn't look happy but when an acquaintance in proximity told me that Yassine didn't have a full time trainer, it was all the excuse I needed to approach the victor as he headed back to the dressing room. The venue was dark save for a spotlight over the ring when I barred his path and asked, "Who trains you...?"

"Nobody," he replied. "I train myself."

"Ok. I am a trainer. I have a license and I would like to work with you."

He looked sceptical but we exchanged numbers and arranged to do a session at the Real Fight Club in a couple of weeks time. He kept the appointment and I quickly discovered that Yassine was basically untrainable in any traditional sense. He had his own modus operandi and didn't trust the mantras of any non participant over the instincts that had been honed by trial and error in the deep end of boxing's shark infested waters. 3 of his 4 losses had come against British fighters who were being groomed for bigger things and he was robbed on each occasion by his own account. He didn't need a trainer to tell him that. He merely sought a good pad man and – better yet – a well connected manager who could broker some meaningful fights, since there was not a light middleweight in the universe to whom he felt subordinate. His seemingly unshakable confidence was vindicated when he dominated future British champion, Anthony Small, in the first sparring session I arranged for him at the gym. I had found a fighter worth getting excited about but plotting an upward trajectory in an industry more bent than Brand's Hatch was always going to be a challenge.

Unfortunately, professional boxing is not founded on the same noble principle as schoolyard conkers. Concepcion was being steered towards titles and television but – having beaten him in devastating fashion – it didn't follow that Yassine had inherited his position. When the away fighter beats the house, his services invariably become less desirable to a promoter as opposed to the reverse. To take a well worn phrase on loan from the late Reg Gutteridge, my new charge was now 'Chairman of the Who Needs Him Club.' Lest I remained oblivious to the facts of life,

Rob McCracken spelled it out to me during a locker room chat:

"Nobody is gonna' look after your kid. You'll just have to keep him fit and hope for the best.."

Still relatively green, I found it all rather exasperating, given Yassine's obvious star potential. He was good looking and charismatic with a fan friendly image and, more importantly, he could fight. In his local area of Hackney he appeared to be the Arab equivalent of Rocky Balboa with everyone from the man in the off license to the revenue protection mob at Homerton station calling his name. To turn him into a ticket seller would hardy require a marketing genius, I contended. Nevertheless, I continued to hear the same token objections whenever I mentioned the name to matchmakers and promoters.

When a late substitute was sought to face a leading domestic light middleweight on the undercard of a big televised show in Manchester, the tragic Dean Powell assured me, "Sky wouldn't approve Yassine as an opponent because of his record." It seemed to be a case of the blind leading the sighted. A significant portion of the blame for the relative decline of a major sport in the 21st century can be laid at the door of an endless procession of clueless TV executives who would struggle to distinguish boxing from badminton. The old sages like legendary Philly promoter J. Russell Peltz understood that "If the TV execs actually had a clue, they would showcase fighters who can fight, even if their records are less than perfect," but the overpaid 'suits' were all about the numbers.

With Britain's premier 154 pounders otherwise engaged, Yassine was given a chance to strut his stuff on Spencer's second ever Hard Knocks promotion at Kensington Town Hall on the last Friday in March. This time we were in the house corner and the imported Latvian opponent seemed largely devoid of fistic merit, save for an almost masochistic durability. Such was his willingness to walk through a tempest of unanswered blows, Dereck Chisora's trainer Don Charles (who happened to be working the corner with me) admitted, "This kid is starting to worry me." There was no cause for alarm as the bell sounded to end the fourth round and our man was duly awarded a 40-35 verdict, signifying a whitewash plus a knockdown in the second stanza. One sided though it might have been, Yassine looked rather electrifying in the precursor to a main event that saw Kresnick Qato's insanely partisan Albanian throng attempt to deafen West London forever. Spencer was piloting a grass roots phenomenon, it seemed, and I had a Moroccan Roy Jones on my hands.

Officially, Yassine had a manager but relations had broken down meaning that the license holder in question simply collected his 25 percent in exchange for doing nothing until the contract expired. Consequently, I began to act unofficially on his behalf as I tried to secure a title fight. Since I'd always had a scathing contempt for the spurious sanctioning body baubles that are used to buy world rankings, I targeted the traditional southern area crown. It so happened that the vacant title at 11 stone had been contested on the night he trounced Concepcion, with Tom Glover winning a 10 round decision over Scott Woolford. My man had already beaten Woolford and I strongly fancied him against Glover but had no idea how such things were mandated.

Being a regulatory body more than a sanctioning body, the Board did not compile official rankings in any division. Title shots under Board jurisdiction were generally awarded via direct lobbying from a fighter's manager or promoter. At this particular time, I also had a light heavyweight who was up for his license application hearing and so – seeking to kill two birds with one stone – I asked the newly appointed area secretary, Les Potts, how I should go about proposing my light middleweight for a southern area title shot. Mr. Potts said he would mention it at the monthly meeting which, rather fortuitously, took place the following day. 24 hours after my casual enquiry, I received a text informing me that Yassine had been approved as a challenger so long as I was able to agree voluntary terms with Glover's team. It all seemed absurdly straight forward but my enthusiasm would be curbed soon enough.

I phoned Frank Maloney, whose number I had gotten from a mutual friend, and found him holidaying in Portugal at the time of the call. He had operated in the uppermost echelon during his days with Lennox Lewis but was now subsisting on the bread and butter of domestic and European level for the most part. Accordingly, he offered to pay £5000 in total for the fight. Next I called Glover's manager, Tony Sims, who told me that the champion would require 5 grand for himself plus expenses. It constituted an impasse and thus the fight was dead in the water. Essentially, the Board had told me to make the match if I could but nobody would lose any sleep in the likely event of my efforts being scuppered. The Area titles had lost their former significance, usurped by a raft of bogus straps with their International, Intercontinental or 'Pentecostal' prefixes. Even the British title had lost much of its gravitas and things would only get worse in years to come.

I wasn't even sure if Yassine was eligible for the British title and I began to have similar doubts about our working relationship. There was nothing disagreeable about his personality but he was rather ungovernable all the same. I believed that the coach was the boss and a fighter ought to follow his instructions like a member of the Manson family. Unfortunately, 'The Showman' was a child of whim and answered to nobody besides himself. Frequently, I would call his mobile only to learn that he was sparring in Manchester, Glasgow or Sheffield in order to supplement his income. I had no control over the situation and it flew in the face of everything I'd ever read about the great trainers and disciplinarians of yore. Perhaps my mindset too possessive but I began to distance myself from the situation as Don Charles took my place as head coach. Before long El Maachi was picked up by the burgeoning Small Hall King, Steve Goodwin, who delivered some TV exposure, culminating in his winning the Matchroom Prizefighter tournament (along with the £32, 000 prize money) in 2011. It should have been the start of a meteoric rise but, for one reason or another, Yassine never fought again and faded into obscurity.

Somewhere, in an alternate universe, I wonder if it all worked out for both of us.

12/ IN BLOOM

Having cut Yassine loose, I was left with Scott Douglas, a teak tough light-heavyweight from Stanford-le-Hope who made up for any paucity of natural talent with a dogged work ethic. He was also a ticket seller in his locale which meant I should be able to get him a few wins whilst assessing his ultimate potential. Actually, the selection of opponents was down to his manager and former Commonwealth cruiserweight champion, Chris Okoh, with whom I had a good rapport having met at Cityboxer. Back then we had shared many a conversation about joining forces and taking over the world although we both realised that Scott Douglas was unlikely to be the fighter who would facilitate such a grand agenda. Regardless, he was the best we had at this particular juncture in time.

Scott debuted at the York Hall in June, beating a tall compliant southpaw named Jamie Norkett on points over 4 rounds. Assisting me in the corner on cuts duty was Dean Powell who basically took over and made it difficult for me to get a word in edgewise during the designated intervals. Being Frank Warren's right hand man, he probably felt entitled to pull rank on another rookie trainer, despite never having taken a punch in his life. The essential bullet points were, "MOVE TO YOUR LEFT AND AIM FOR HIS CHEST" which was sound enough advice against an opponent who brought all the ambition and vibrancy of a tear stained suicide note. Although the opposition was undemanding, Scott looked surprisingly polished which duly created the impression that I was responsible for the transformation. The show took place on a Sunday afternoon and I was enjoying the backslaps from his boozy army of well wishers in the Dundee Arms – a claustrophobically small pub opposite the venue – when the ambience was ruined by an unpunctual emergency.

Diana had been rushed into Homerton Hospital with irregular bleeding and Joseph was at her mother's. Naturally, there were fears that she may be on the verge of a miscarriage or perhaps another premature delivery but I simply resented the timing of the debacle. For some reason, I decided that the most expedient course of action was to buy a bottle of Southern Comfort before plotting up at the flat in Maitland Road and watching hours of Benny Leonard footage on YouTube. I didn't check on the well-being of my significant other until just after midnight, having gotten a lift to the hospital from her sister's boyfriend. By that point I was insensibly drunk and incapable of offering any reassurance whatsoever. For the avoidance of doubt, let it be said that I was a lousy partner to Diana and any lasting enmity she may have forged is entirely understandable. Fortunately, there was no miscarriage and she was discharged the next day.

After a rent increase at the Real Fight Club, I moved my base to Rooney's Gym on Bermondsey Street, a stone's throw from London Bridge station. The owner, John Rooney, was an Irishman who had initially launched the business as a London franchise of Gleason's but the alliance was short lived for whatever reason. Despite his reputation for being the kind of guy who wanted all the oxygen in a lift, I found him a lovable rogue in the main. As a manager and trainer, he had taken Martin Lindsay to the British featherweight title and also enjoyed a degree of success with the gregarious East End heavyweight, Micky Steeds. At the time of our acquaintance, he had a small stable of novice pros including black Bristolian, Darren Hamilton, who was unbeaten in 5 starts before a 2 year hiatus that saw him move to London and seek to establish himself as a personal trainer. Disillusioned with the fight game, he was coming back chiefly because his employment at the gym had been contingent on the signing of a 3 year managerial contract.

Another fighter based at the gym was Darren Sutherland, the red hot Irish super middleweight prospect who had beaten James DeGale in 4 of 6 amateur fights despite coming second best in their Olympic semi – final. Tipped to go all the way in the paid ranks, the lofty expectations proved more than his muscular shoulders could bear as the mixed race prodigy was found hanged in his Beckenham digs by a distraught Frank Maloney who suffered a minor heart attack on sight. Rumours abounded that Darren wanted to quit the game but was under heavy pressure to honour his contractual obligations, not to mention an alleged £75, 000 investment from the diminutive promoter. Sutherland and his coach, Bryan Lawrence, had also trained at the Real Fight Club during which time I had the formed impression that he was a highly driven individual who relished the life of a top prospect in the spotlight. At the risk of descending into the realm of cliche, he just didn't seem the type to take his own life. Almost 3 years later, a coroner endorsed that perception and returned an open verdict whilst conceding that the deceased may have been 'too sensitive and intelligent' to be a boxer.

2 weeks after Darren's untimely demise, Lucas Benjamin Doughty entered the world at 11.17am on Thursday October 1, to the strains of 'Nirvana'. A small radio in the theatre was blaring an array of popular songs when my second son appeared during the chorus of 'In Bloom', which seemed apt if not classically romantic. In sync with the soundtrack, I felt strangely neutral as if the trauma of Joseph's birth and subsequent journey had put a safety catch on my emotions. Nonetheless, mother and baby were home within days and I soon came to adore Lucas as Diana and I got on with the business of being a mismatched couple with a young family. There was an asterisk over Joseph's development as he was slow to walk and yet to talk, leading to ripples of concern that he was 'on the spectrum.' It was troubling but nothing that my nightly consumption of beer and liquor couldn't suppress for the time being.

On the first day of December, I got a call from Mickey Helliet offering me a fight for Scott Douglas that same evening on his annual dinner show at the Sheraton Hotel. At this point, Scott had fallen out with Chris Okoh, leaving me as the sole decision maker in such matters. The opponent, one Stefan Hughes, had been blitzed in 40 seconds by Birtley hot shot, Travis Dickinson, in his only previous professional appearance. It seemed too good to be true; an easy opponent for a guaranteed purse with no ticket obligation, out of the blue. I persuaded Scott to take the fight and he signed a contract at the venue which named Helliet as the his manager for the next 24 hours. Underestimating Hughes based on a single stoppage loss turned out to be a mistake as Scott was dropped like a ton of bricks in the second round from a counter right hand that sounded like a shotgun blast. Gamely he rosé and did his best to narrow the gap but a knockdown in a 4 rounder is tantamount to sudden death and the referee's verdict of 39-37 in favour of the Welsh fighter came as no surprise.

With his unbeaten record being forfeited for the amusement of a half interested crowd of ball gowns and tuxedoes, I couldn't help feeling that I had let my fighter down. Hughes had been blown away on his debut but that didn't make him a proven loser who knew how to play the game. When the bell rang he fought like a man possessed and it was us who were served up for dessert under the chandeliers. Scott and I didn't fall out but drifted apart thereafter and it would be 4 and half years before he boxed again. After 18 months as a licensed professional trainer, it was evident that I struggled to maintain a relationship with a fighter and was losing my illusions about a business that looked infinitely more glamorous from an agreeable distance, filtered through the medium of television.

The fighter/ trainer dynamic wasn't the only relationship I struggled to maintain as Diana kicked me out 2 days before Christmas. Reluctant to bother friends at such a time of year, with John Rooney's blessing, I holed up in the gym and slept on the sofa in the downstairs reception area. I was feeling decidedly sorry for myself on Christmas morning when I posted a causal S.O.S on Facebook outlining my predicament whilst trying not to sound desperate. Spencer came to the rescue and invited me to his mother's flat in Kennington where I was plied with food, alcohol and the near hypnotic positivity that he always seemed to exude. As a devout Muslim, he didn't celebrate the former pagan festival nor indulge in strong potations but he was able to source a liberal amount of Guinness and London Dry Gin to which I was instructed to help myself. We watched a DVD of the Mike McCallum – Sean Mannion fight and a rare Muhammad Ali interview from the 60s before he spoke of his grand plans for the future. Much of what he predicted that afternoon came true in spectacular fashion although I wouldn't understand the process that enabled such things for many years.

He was speaking his dreams into existence, aided by an unshakeable faith in a higher power. Everything was going wrong for me because, being in the throes of addiction, I was spiritually bankrupt. I had no security or peace of mind and in spite of my ambition to be become a trainer of champions, everything played second fiddle to my fixation with the booze. I had nowhere to live and was terrified of becoming estranged from my children, replaced by a more reliable suitor. Rather than face my fears head on, I cloaked them in ego and vanity, doggedly refusing to grow up and deal with the enemy within. With such a mindset, it was inevitable that any enlightened counsel was going to fall on deaf ears.

You can lead a horse to water but you can't stop it from drinking.

13/ AMMO

Darren Hamilton and I had a lot in common. We both lived comically haphazard lives on a hand to mouth basis and - like me - he had also found himself at the mercy of Rooney's benevolence. For months he had slept in the gym before a disagreement between the two of them led to his dismissal into the big blue yonder. Down on our mutual luck at the beginning of 2010, we moved into a house in Catford that was little better than derelict but marginally preferable to the cold outdoors. Having procured a roof over our heads, I took Darren to the 'Fight Club' and introduced him to Spencer. I explained that my friend was undefeated and had the potential to be a champion if properly nurtured and given an opportunity. Always willing to help a brother in need, Spencer got him a job at the gym and placed his new light welterweight prospect under the tutelage of Harry Andrews, who immediately set about transforming a lazy recreational drug user into a championship calibre fighter.

As profound as the transformation was, the fairy tale comeback did not proceed without an initial hiccup at Goresbrook Leisure Centre on a crisp night in March. Spencer had gotten our man a 4 rounder on the undercard of a double header in Dagenham featuring Matthew Hatton's bid for the European Welterweight crown and a British light middleweight title clash between Sam Webb and the controversial Anthony Small. The show was promoted by Matthew's older brother and British boxing legend, Ricky, who was looking to establish a power base on the safe of the ropes after his devastating loss to Manny Pacquaio. The tone for a luckless evening was set when Darren almost got nicked at Tottenham Hale station whilst attempting to traverse the barriers without paying. Harry was aghast and amused in equal measure that he would jeopardise a fight on a major televised card for the sake of a couple of quid but diplomacy prevailed and we were allowed to continue on our way.

When we arrived at the venue, Yassine El Maachi was embroiled in a heated discussion with matchmaker, Richard Poxon, regarding the scheduling of his fight and whether it would be filmed. Sky TV shows often featured bouts known as 'floaters' that could take place at any time - and occasionally didn't happen at all - depending on time slot requirements. Bizarrely, Yassine was insisting that he should not be recorded in action, perhaps due to the standard nature of his purse. "WHY would you not want to be filmed...?" wondered Poxon, clearly unacquainted with the peculiar 'Showman' logic. Darren went on at around 9pm and it was providential that the ensuing catastrophe was not captured in moving pictures.

For 11 and a half minutes, he stood the limited but dangerous Daryl Setterfield on his head before a lapse in concentration saw him get dramatically 'sparked' in the dying seconds. A Hall Mary left hook found its target, causing Darren's impossibly skinny legs to betray him as the away fighter followed up with a hail of blows from which only the kitchen sink was conspicuously absent. It was what those in the know call a 'bad knockout' and concerns for Darren's safety were magnified when he appeared to have a borderline psychotic episode backstage. Jumping around the changing room and ranting unintelligibly about his opponent's unforgivable weight advantage he resisted all attempts at a post fight examination by the Board doctor. Seeking to placate the stricken fighter, Southern Area Chairman Mick Collier interjected:

"MARK... CALM DOWN...! ALL WE CARE ABOUT IS THAT YOU ARE STILL HERE TOMORROW.."

I pointed out that his name was Darren but my clarification went unheeded as Mr. Collier continued to stress, "WE'RE ON YOUR SIDE, MARK, RELAX...!" Eventually, a calm was established and 'Mark' submitted to the standard questions of Who, Where and What before going to Newham Hospital for precautionary observation. Harry asked me to go with him but I considered it his responsibility as head coach and had another obligation in any case.

Anthony Small's trainer, Dave Pereira, had asked me to hand up to him in the co main event and, naturally, I accepted with glee. Although I would be little more than a glorified bucket boy, my face would be seen live on Sky Sports and my name would appear in graphics on the screen. Not for me the tag of humble servant in the shadows, I wanted the spotlight and the glory. Unfortunately, there would be little glory attached to the defending champion's name in the years that followed but - without the gift of clairvoyance - I was hardly to know. Anthony had never been a ticket seller and although he was technically the house fighter, being signed to Hatton promotions, the paying audience was decidedly pro Webb. It seemed reasonable to expect a hostile reception as we walked to the ring but Ambrose Mendy had a plan.

Perhaps the most beguiling character I have met in the fight game, Ambrose had burst onto the scene in the late 80s as Nigel Benn's self styled Svengali. A master of hype and ceremony with an extraordinary gift of the gab his chief talent lay in exploiting the layman's perceptions. I entered the squash court that approximated Small's dressing room and found him watching Roy Jones videos on a portable DVD player whilst an Islamic prayer recording played in the background. Warming up in view of the Sky cameras was a young black man of similar stamp and stature to the British light middleweight champion dressed in a hooded black satin robe and the 'Scream' mask that had hitherto been Anthony's trademark. It was enough to fool Ricky Hatton's mum when, flanked by myself and Dave Pereira, the imposter made his way through the tunnel and received an affectionate pat on the back. "GOOD LUCK, ANTHONY LOVE...!"

We entered the arena and soaked up the boos and jeers from the well represented 'UKIP' faction in the stands and then - as we approached the ring - the doppelgänger suddenly turned and ran back to the dressing room as if overcome by a last minute bout of stage fright. Dave and I mounted the steps as he shrugged in

Ricky Hatton's direction, who smirked uneasily and said, "I don't know what the fuck you lot are up to." Webb's ample supporters had just screamed themselves hoarse, hurling insults at a man who worked as an estate agent from Monday to Friday. When the real Anthony Small made his entrance, cutting a resplendent figure in a white Velcro Adidas track suit and trilby, they seemed to have nothing left. Although not seen by the viewers at home, Ambrose had won the opening round.

As the fight got underway, I felt a little disappointed with Small, who was a potentially world class fighter when firing on all cylinders. He was winning - or so I thought - but not exactly shining in the process and seemed to be favouring one shot at a time as opposed to the blistering combinations he was capable of putting together. Although Webb was doing better then we might have anticipated both Dave and I were surprised when Richard Poxon approached the corner during the tenth round and warned, "Sky have got it level." The 11 and 12th were close but the whole momentum seemed to be building in favour of Webb. One could feel it in the air.

Richie Davies gave it to the challenger by 4 points whilst Marcus McDonnell had them all square. Ian John Lewis, who might have given Custer a draw at Little Big Horn, scored 117-112 in favour of .....'THE WINNER BY MAJORITY DECISION....AND THE NEW BRITISH LIGHT MIDDLEWEIGHT CHAMPION....' As Webb's fans voiced their raucous approval, it occurred me to that professional boxing in the 21st century is essentially a popularity contest as much as anything else. And nobody much cared for a brash, cocky Muslim who could scarcely have expected any favours if the blue eyed boy was still standing at the final bell. As Sam celebrated in the ring with his trainer, Alan Smith, I wondered if the latter remembered our encounter on the Old Kent Road, 7 years earlier. Probably not I concluded as we filed back to the changing room without hanging around for the post fight interview.

What ought to have been a relatively minor setback became a death knell as Anthony Small never fought again. Apparently radicalised by Islamic extremists, he garnered tabloid attention 3 months later whilst attending a protest against British soldiers who had recently returned from Afghanistan, during a parade in Barking, East London. The soldiers had been denounced as murderers and reportedly spat upon although Small refuted the secondary accusation. In boxing circles, his name remains worse than mud to this day with only his relative anonymity precluding wider vilification on the streets of South London where he allegedly still lives.

By contrast, Darren rose from the ashes of the Setterfield glitch and went on to win the British light welterweight title with 3 days notice on a fabulous night in Liverpool in the spring of 2012. In the wake of his triumph, much was made by the trade press of the 'Homeless to Hero' angle, although there were no fortunes to be made at domestic level outside of the heavyweight division. The important thing was that my belief at the outset had been vindicated and Spencer had his first major champion. A contentious split decision loss to footballer turned boxer, Curtis Woodhouse, would eventually prevent him from making the Lonsdale Belt his permanent property but at least Mick Collier would know his name by then. In a subculture that regards cerebral damage and insolvency as par for the course, it could have been worse.

14/ FAST EDDIE AND THE PRIZEFIGHTER

Despite the ludicrously good looks and imposing stature, he almost blended into the background in 2011. Having not then accrued the global eminence that would come his way, Edward John Hearn was only known to the interested parties assembled for the International Heavyweight Prizefighter weigh in on the upper landing of the Tower Bridge Hotel. There were no hordes of internet media hanging on his every word and only a smattering of tourists gazed quizzically as the near naked behemoths stepped on and off the scales. In a short space of time he would become inaccessible to anyone without a press accreditation and a wealth of patience - assuming they were not counted amongst the big hitters in accordance with the holy grail of YouTube views.

His father Barry - Chairman and founder of the Matchroom Sport colossus - had all but lost interest in boxing when young Eddie proposed to spearhead the Renaissance. A chance meeting with Audley Harrison in Las Vegas circa 2009 - whist looking after the family poker arm - led to a pact in their mutual interest and the rest is history. The big man was relaunched as a credible contender by virtue of winning the European crown before capitulating to David Haye in arguably the most passive world heavyweight title challenge in the annals of the sport. As pitiful as it was, the human sacrifice attracted an estimated quarter of a million pay per view customers on Sky Box Office and the Eddie Hearn phenomenon was underway.

Immediately prior to his come from behind victory over Michael Sprott for the EBU strap, Harrison had won the 8th instalment of the popular 'Prizefighter' tournament for which a collection of walking juggernauts was now assembled. The TV friendly format became the linchpin of the first phase of the Matchroom comeback; 8 fighters, 7 fights, 1 winner and 32 'bags of sand' for the last man standing. Some of the purists balked at the notion of professional fighters in 3 round fights but at least everybody was trying to win. The story had a beginning, middle and end that seldom failed to provide drama and controversy. It was compulsive viewing for the diehards and casuals alike.

Undefeated Lucian Bot was intending to spend the prize money on a house in Bucharest to share with his lovely fiancé who was studying for a PHD in chemistry. A few days earlier his Lancashire based manager, Sam Betts, had reached out to me on Facebook and asked if I would look after his man until he was able to join us at the weekend. A successful businessman who had been around the fight game for decades, Sam had recently read 'The Secret' and was seeking my help in accordance with the law of attraction. By this point, I had built quite a following on social media and was gaining credence as an authority on all matters boxing but, in truth, he was the one helping me out.

On the night, at the Alexandra Palace, the magnitude of the occasion seemed to have gotten the better of our handsome Romanian hopeful. He complained about the hand wraps, despite Sam's meticulous binding, and seemed a little fazed by the proximity of Michael Sprott and Cuban favourite, Mike Perez, in the communal dressing room. Admittedly, Sprott's warm up routine was unlikely to strike fear into the hearts of potential adversaries as he tapped the pads so lightly that it might have passed for a Swedish massage technique. "They're not giving anything away," Sam whispered. In another part of the room, Jim Evans was casually debunking the legend of Henry Cooper. "I saw him a few times," explained the grey haired Berkshire boxing doyen. "Not the best and never the bravest but he dined out on that one punch." Lucian's arse might have gone but I was loving every minute of the experience, as always.

In the quarter final we drew Konstantin Airich, who compensated for a lack of finesse with a thudding clout in both mitts. His brawling, uncultured aggression forced our man to take a count in the first round which effectively signed his death warrant on the scorecards. Lucian came back well in the second and third, showing heart and a good chin but it wasn't enough to make up the deficit. "STAY WITH YOUR MAN, BEN...!" warned Sam, aware that my attention was distracted by one of the round card girls as we left the ring. Head bowed in mourning for his unbeaten record, Lucian was several paces ahead of me as he trudged back towards the changing rooms. Quickening my stride, I caught up with him whilst Sam went in search of the money. Losing in the first series was worth 4 grand and all purses were paid in cash on the night. Aside from the useful exposure, I was given £300 for my input which seemed more than fair.

One of the eminently wonderful things about the Matchroom set up was the no holds barred hospitality. Hotel guests during company events were permitted to order anything besides champagne and hookers and the bill was always honoured. "Drink what you like tonight, Ben," Sam advised. Opting to get on the road back to Preston with his family, he left me the room key and his blessing to run up a bar tab in the name of Mr. Betts. Requiring very little in the way of encouragement, I wound up drinking until 5am in the morning with losing finalist, Tye Fields, and his incongruously young coach. Tye had put paid to Airich was a crippling body shot in the first round before being blitzed in 42 seconds of the final by Perez whom he utterly dwarfed - albeit to no avail. The last thing I could remember was a pact being made to watch the Manny Pacquiao- Shane Mosley fight talking place in Vegas that same night before waking up to the sound of a vacuum cleaner being manoeuvred around me, slumped as I was in a hardback chair. On such occasions, there was always a knee jerk sense of stigma as I imagined my impromptu drinking buddies tiptoeing away from the scene and shaking their heads wistfully, perhaps remarking that it was 'a shame' because I seemed like 'a nice guy.'

A month later, at the weigh in for the Welterweight Prizefighter in the same venue, I became aware of a new presence that would become widely synonymous with British boxing in the

21st century. A large man of Asian extraction with an Essex Boy demeanour could be seen interviewing the fighters and assorted principles with a hand held camera and microphone. His name was given as Kugan Cassius and the word was that he'd previously had a gig as Ricky Hatton's body guard. The content was apparently for a YouTube channel called 'iFILM London' and he was partnered in the venture by friend and sidekick, James Helder. The ground breaking former female fighter, Jane Couch, had also been added to the fold in the interests of colour and charisma. Kugan's own interviewing style was rather dry and lethargic and I was tempted to conclude that whole enterprise wouldn't amount to much but my instincts could not have been more spectacularly wrong.

Kugan struck gold in the zeitgeist of boxing reportage in the social media age as iFILM London evolved into iFLTV with the backing of the controversial Irish powerhouse MTK and sponsorship from the likes of William Hill. He and Eddie Hearn effectively morphed into a double act, each feeding off the other and creating a culture that soon saw pressers and weigh ins besieged by a hundred aspiring bloggers, all seeking to emulate the success and blueprint of the mighty IFL. Some of the old hacks from the establishment press were galled by the low brow anarchy of it all but it was a natural progression in the digital age of instant gratification. I don't doubt that Schulberg and Liebling were spinning in their graves.

The Featherweight Prizefighter took place at York Hall on October 29 and, again, I had a vested interest due to my relationship with a fighter's management. Despite being told by all and sundry that he would never be an attraction in the UK, Spencer Fearon and Ciaran Baynes saw something in a marauding Mongolian by the name of Choi Tseveenpurev and threw the weight of Hard Knocks behind him. Known to British fans for his annihilation of Derry Matthews for the spurious WBU title, Choi seemed to get frozen out until he came under Spencer's wing in

2009. I had been in his corner 5 months earlier for a 10 round points win over the useful Jackson Asiku in a small hall classic and many of those in attendance had clearly been converted to the cult of the Mongol Warrior.

By this time, I had left Rooney's in favour of TKO Gym, located on an industrial estate in Canning Town. The guvnor, Johnny Eames, trained and managed a large stable of fighters out of a space that contained 3 boxing rings on the upper floor of a building that housed a printing press downstairs. It was the quintessential unpretentious East London fight factory that saw plenty of 'names' passing through its doors on a regular basis. Johnny also happened to have a kid in the Prizefighter called George Jupp which led to some vaguely good natured banter casting me as the enemy. In truth, I never felt fully accepted by the clique at the best of times since I wasn't a cab driver or a villain and I'd never been a 'street kid' as Johnny often saw fit to remind me. The one person I did feel akin to was the legendary Jimmy Tibbs with whom I forged a firm friendship from innumerable hours of passionate conversations about boxing past and present.

As the tournament commenced, Choi swept aside the overmatched Lee Glover without breaking sweat before coming up against Jupp in the semi final. Team TKO won the first battle backstage when we lost the coin toss to determine which of the fighters would be permitted to wear his favoured red and blue trunks. But trunks don't win fights and although George put in an admirable shift for a fresh faced novice against a dangerous world class featherweight, the verdict in Choi's favour was not controversial. "Never in a million years..!" growled Johnny Eames in a touching display of myopic loyalty as both teams met in ring centre for the protocol of congratulation and commiseration. He would not have relished losing to me and Spencer and preferred to believe in a miscarriage of justice.

The touted Rhys Roberts who bore the sobriquet of 'Pure Silk' couldn't handle Choi's suffocating pressure and lost every round on each of the judges' cards in a final might have been anti-climactic to the neutral spectator. At the precise moment John McDonald announced the winner, I hoisted Choi aloft on my shoulders and hoped the Sky cameras were capturing my vicarious triumph. Once back on terra firma, Choi lifted the trophy and broke into song - as was his habit - while Eddie Hearn shook my hand and offered, "Well done, mate." In truth, I hadn't really done anything since Choi had pretty much trained himself but my Facebook wall was awash with plaudits and allusions to a 'tactical masterplan' of which I was plainly the architect. Full to the brim with false pride, it was time to celebrate once more at Matchroom's expense.

Having no use for his complimentary hotel room at the Shoreditch Crowne Plaza , Spencer had given the key to a young Scottish fighter of my acquaintance who went by the name of Jamie 'Smigga' Smith. Actually, he was known to use various aliases and turned out to be a pure fantasist but he wasn't bad company if one could ignore the intricately woven back story. Signing for copious libations in the name of Fearon, we got drunk and hung out on the roof as I basked in the reflective glory of Choi's great victory. Although I didn't receive a penny for my duties in the corner, the resultant bar tab was probably on a par with Freddie Roach's fee for a 10 rounder. When I awoke on the Sunday morning, a hair of the dog was the only plausible strategy worth considering. Desperate as ever to maintain the buzz of my grandiose illusions, a hangover was simply not an option.

On the pads with Alfie at Angel ABC, circa 2004

With the late Frankie Fraser at the Repton on the same day I first met Sugar Ray Leonard , October 2005

THROWING IN THE TOWEL

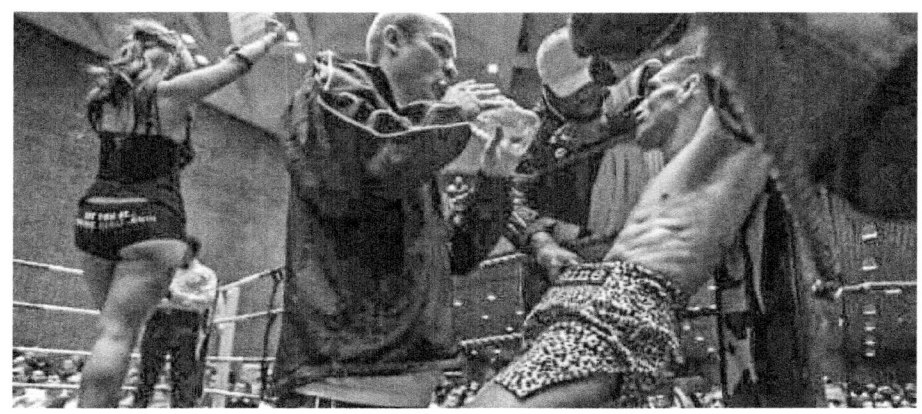

Helping myself to a swig of the 'Showman's water. Kensington Town Hall, October 2009

Choi wins the Prizefighter, October 2011

With Darren Hamilton at the Liverpool Echo Arena after the second defence of his British Light-Welterweight crown.

The 'Mongol Warrior' immediately after his fight with John Simpson at the Glasgow Emirates Arena in 2013

THROWING IN THE TOWEL

Roy Jones lays down the law to myself and Ben Day, Las Vegas 2014

BEN DOUGHTY

Feeling 16 years old again with 'Iron Mike' in Sin City

Uncle Frank has a bone to pick with me at a press conference in February 2015

With my ultimate ring hero in a bookshop basement, March 2012

With Alex Morrison immediately after the interview that caused all the trouble

With big Frank at Hunt's Lounge in Chessington. Another financial disaster....!

THROWING IN THE TOWEL

With my brother from another mother, as he might say. Spencer Fearon AKA
'Master Knowledge'

On stage with the 'Dark Destroyer' at the Prince Regent Chigwell, October 2015

THROWING IN THE TOWEL

I always got the feeling that Nigel could take me or leave me

Backstage at York Hall with Robert Asagba on the night of his professional debut

With the great Jimmy Tibbs at West Ham ABC while the barber tries to look busy

With Michael Watson 'The People's Champion', November 2015

THROWING IN THE TOWEL

Larry seemed more interested in my girlfriend than anything I had to say. York Hall, November 2013

With Shaun on the German Excursion From Hell. Dusseldorf 2015

THROWING IN THE TOWEL

With Anthony Joshua at West Ham after a life shortening bender

The legendary Tony Burns at his spiritual home in 2017

THROWING IN THE TOWEL

With the 'Pitbull' at the 02 Arena for the Anthony Joshua – Charles Martin fight in April 2016

Back on good terms with 'Fast Eddie', September 2017

15/ SUGARTOWN

My tenure at the Catford hovel only lasted a few weeks after which I led an increasingly nomadic existence, comprising a blizzard of temporary addresses and various attempts to get back with Diana and make a go of things. I remained involved with the kids - the day-care, the nursery runs and bath times - and would frequently sleep on the sofa at Maitland Road whether I had an official residence or not. It was at this point that life took on a truly dichotomous bent, with my social media celebrity and proximity to the great and good standing in stark contrast to the short lived house shares and alcoholic instability. The first major breakthrough in the former regard came on March 13, 2012.

Sugar Ray Leonard - himself a recovering alcoholic - was in London to promote his autobiography 'The Big Fight' and Spencer suggested I chance my arm and try to get an interview with him. We had recently launched a weekly magazine show on YouTube (before anyone else was doing it) but he was unable to get to the studio on this particular day due to another obligation. A sit down chat with the Sugarman would compensate for his absence, he modestly proposed. Although 'The Spirit' was a charismatic and well connected presence in the industry he didn't quite have the kind of cachet to command an audience with one of the most iconic living fighters in the world. When I rolled up for the midday book signing at the Canary Wharf branch of Waterstones with co - producer and camera-girl in tow, I did so with considerable temerity.

Strategy would obviously be of great import. I decided against buying a copy of the book and joining the endless queue of fans on the mezzanine, gravitating instead towards the table at which the main man was seated. I identified the lady who was in charge of the afternoon's agenda and introduced myself, waxing lyrical about the huge and fictitious traction of 'Doughty And The Spirit' amongst UK boxing fans. She was young and attractive and - unlike most of her gatekeeping ilk - seemed perfectly amenable to my audacious request at the very least. Like a fresh faced intern on her first day at the office, she replied, "Ok. If you can email the details to me, I will show it to him when we break for lunch at one and see if he wants to do it."

I fired off an email from my blackberry and, unsure of what to do next, we hung around watching the great man scrawling signatures and posing for pictures with a continual procession of star struck admirers. He was clad in an egoless pale blue shirt and jeans, with only an ostentatiously large gold watch betraying any sign of foreboding wealth. A flicker of hope arrived in the shape of former GB coach, Terry Edwards, who stumbled on the scene apparently by pure coincidence having not known that Sugar Ray was in town. I knew Terry, who was evidently acquainted with the legend at whom he made a convivial hand gesture and shouted, "Ray.. Phone me…" Since they were such good buddies, might he be our conduit, I wondered…? "I imagine he will be inundated, don't you…?" shrugged Terry before continuing to wherever he was headed in the first place.

At 1pm sharp, my idol was ushered away by a pair of Eastern European looking goons who kept the stragglers at bay with a churlish menace. We grabbed a spot of lunch in an effort to kill the clock but there was still no sign of the golden email when we repaired to Canning Town an hour later, bereft of optimism. Back at the gym, the incidental presence of tabloid celebrity, Alex Reid, seemed to rub salt in the wound of my disappointment. A friend called and kept me talking for the best part of half an hour and only when I hung up did I discover the communication from Mr. Leonard's publicist. Sugar Ray was agreeable to an interview provided we could be at the Leadenhall Street branch of Waterstones for 4.45pm. Frantically, I informed Davie and Louise that we had precisely 40 minutes to transit from East London to The City and there was no time for sloth or procrastination.

The first hurdle came when the ticket machine at Star Lane

DLR regurgitated my paper currency 3 times on the spin before I elected to board the next train without paying. Changing at West Ham, we continued to Monument station where I vaulted the barriers and yelled, "Sorry but I'm late for an interview with SUGAR RAY 'FUCKING' LEONARD...!" The Afro Caribbean gentleman employed to prevent such anarchy appeared to understand as the three of us pelted into the rush hour streets like an Olympic relay team. It was 4.44pm when we arrived at the store, outside which an extensive queue had formed as the City types began to spill out of their offices. "There you are...! I've been looking for you," said the pretty PR lady before escorting us through a side entrance and down into the basement where the sour faced goons stood, barring the threshold. One of them - be it tweedle dum or tweedle dee - seemed disquieted by Davie's alternative tattooed appearance and conceded our access to the superstar with visible reluctance.

Following our exertions, we were sufficiently sweat drenched for the Sugarman to enquire, "What happened to you guys...?! Have you been running...?" Briefly, I relayed to him the details of our swashbuckling commute - including the necessary fare evasion - while stressing, "There is not another fighter, living or dead, that I would do this for." (That was a lie, in fact, since I would also have done it for Muhammad Ali.) After breaking the ice with a question about his loss as a teenager in the 1972 Olympic Trials, I asked how much of his style had been an homage to Ali...? With the ice cool delivery that was his trademark, he dropped the biro he had been playing with and confessed, "It was a process.. When I first started boxing I was 14 and I tried to emulate Joe Frazier."

On the subject of Angelo Dundee, he admitted, "People don't know this but Angie didn't train me per se. He would come in 2 weeks prior to a fight. There were a lot of disagreements between Mike Trainer and Angelo Dundee but all that mattered was that Angelo and I were dear friends. I went to see him 2 weeks prior to his passing and we remained very close." More revelations ensued before I asked if he felt a sense of peace having penned such a reputedly warts and all memoir:

"Oh, I'm glad you said that. A sense of peace.. a sense of calm. I didn't think I'd be as transparent and open as I have been in this book - with the revelations about sexual abuse and my drugs and alcohol...accessibility. But listen, I did it, I'm not proud of it.. I got it off my chest. I'm here in London meeting beautiful fans.. Life is great now."

My 15 minutes expired in the blink of an eye but I would spend the next several months obsessively watching the YouTube upload whilst simultaneously seeking to make my pancreas explode. When I eventually destroyed the laptop by virtue of passing out with a glass of whisky and coke in my hand it seemed akin to the parable of Narcissus, who died ogling his own reflection.

Late night mishaps aside, I did my best to hide the excessive midweek drinking from my new flat mate. 10 years earlier it had been a badge of honour but it suddenly occurred to me that most well adjusted adults didn't relish the idea of living with a person who was perpetually spannered after 7pm. Consequently, I would often drink in my room instead of the lounge at our lovely 2 bedroom flat in the affluent suburb of Wanstead. 'Widget' liked a beer and a bird as much as the next red blooded young man but he also had a proper job with a salary and soon became disillusioned with my chaotic idea of what constituted a bachelor pad. The arrangement would last 9 months before he bailed after the disappearance of an historically expensive bottle of rare blended whisky. Actually, the bottle didn't disappear at all but the contents did and that appeared to be the deal breaker. Like everyone else, he had discovered that I was vastly more likeable from the regular distance of casual acquaintance.

Meanwhile, I was in sexual purgatory. Although the relationship was a charred corpse, it took me years to effectively split from Diana and to separate my love for Joseph and Lucas from any feelings I still harboured for her. Small wonder then that my dalliances were short lived while the emotional confusion persisted. In addition to facilitating interviews with all time great welterweights, Facebook introduced me to a series of superficially attractive but rather desperate women who would have made Glenn Close's character in 'Fatal Attraction' appear standoffish. Helen from Peterborough was blonde and curvaceous but clingy and afraid of escalators. Tracy from Dublin - also blonde - jumped on a plane for a first date in the summer and turned in a performance worthy of a 1970s porn star at the back of the National Express coach from Stansted to Stratford. Like fast food deliveries to the libido, both came to stay at the Wanstead penthouse for 3 days after which I was bombarded with messages that would have been more explicable had I reneged on a promise to marry the pair of them.

Janine was different. One Sunday evening in October, an online dialogue commenced that was notable for its abject lack of luridness. Instantly, I could tell that she was a classy lady who wouldn't contemplate the casual brazenness of sending risqué photographs to a man she had never met before. Pleasantries were engaged and a date was made for the following Saturday night in her native Chelmsford but there were no premature declarations of lust or plans to set sail on the Venetian Lagoon. At her suggestion, we plumped for the more prosaic setting of The Railway pub near Witham Station where she had already arranged to gather with friends. It was a scenario that provided an easy escape route if either one of us turned out to be less than enchanted with the reality behind the Facebook visage.

On the night, my trek was impeded by the mandatory weekend transport diversions but when I eventually arrived at the half full tavern, it was evident that Janine was at least 5 times as stunning as her perfectly agreeable profile pictures.

She expressed embarrassment at having dragged me to such a godforsaken dive and berated the 'awful music' before I went to the bar and got us a drink. Thereafter, we spent the next 3 hours embroiled in conversation, sufficiently engrossing that I only drank 3 pints of lager throughout the whole evening. My regular M.O was to ply my intended prey with booze in the hope that carnality would follow but there was something about this alluring mixed race girl with the penetrating brown eyes that compelled a man to up his game. She wasn't rampantly flirtatious but we seemed to have a chemistry and when I returned from the gents and overheard her asking a friend if she was in possession of chewing gum, I took it as a good sign

At closing time, being as I was stranded in the wilds of Essex, she invited me back to her place along with a chaperone called Lorna. In deference to the old maxim that three is a crowd - and perhaps noticing our conjoined hands in the back of the taxi - Lorna made her excuses and asked the driver to drop her off en route. Minus the gooseberry, we arrived at a cute new build house in a sleepy cul-de-sac and were soon canoodling on the couch, intermittently swapping snippets of verbal autobiographies. That night there was intimacy without intercourse and much of the next day was spent chatting in bed with the life affirming, carefree abandon that characterises a fresh romantic liaison.

For our next date, a few days later in Wanstead, she arrived clad in black, appearing even more radiant than she had in her natural habitat. An Indian takeaway was succeeded by more tantalising foreplay as the seeds of obsession continued to be sewn. Date 3 was fatal, with the essential bullet points of a demure white cocktail dress and a Muhammad Ali box set that she presented to me as a gift. Before long, we were officially an item and even the tritest of songs on the radio was suddenly invested with a heart tugging significance. Inevitably, there was a honeymoon period of all consuming dandiness before the downside reared its ugly head once more. Janine was a good time girl who enjoyed a few Malibu and cokes but she wasn't an alcoholic and she didn't especially desire to be with one. She was interested in travel, eating out, socialising and making strides in her professional life. Despite masquerading as a major player in the fight game, I was chiefly interested in getting drunk and having sex. I didn't relish being out with her in public and was aggressively possessive in response to the copious male attention she received. Arguments erupted and pubs or clubs were hastily exited as I struggled to acknowledge that I had become the kind of boyfriend that I'd always held a scathing contempt for.

In truth, of course, I was so madly in love that it scared me.

16/ THE DRUGS DON'T WORK

When Widget made good his escape in January 2013, the landlady refused to continue the tenancy, leaving me once again without fixed abode. Janine consented to the storage of my less essential belongings in her loft but was too smart to let me move in, which would have been my natural recourse in the event of no resistance. After a few weeks of couch surfing, I found a house-share in Haringey Green Lanes and got on with the business of drinking myself into a probable early grave. Every day I would resolve to lay off the sauce that night only to find myself heading to pub or off license as if manipulated by some evil puppeteer when dusk encroached. Every now and then, I would be so sickeningly chastised by the hangovers that I would abstain for 3 or 4 days but it never lasted. As soon as the 'shivering denizen' got the spring back in his step, I would revert to type.

As previously stated, in addition to the brittle nature of my romantic and residential affairs, I was struggling to maintain a relationship with a professional fighter. With Jack, Scott and Yassine it had been one thing or another but Frankie Monkhouse was the first boxer to unambiguously leave me. Originally from Greenock, Frank came from fighting stock with his father of the same name having briefly boxed as a pro bantamweight in the mid 1980s. He was hugely likeable and utterly dedicated with just one minor drawback; he simply didn't have the requisite talent to progress beyond the level of a 6 round fighter. Nonetheless, he afforded me a presence in the game and racked up 3 wins against away corner fodder before running into a Latvian import who hadn't read the script.

Perhaps a glossary of terms would be useful at this point. A journeyman is a capable fighter who comes to do a job of work without upsetting the apple cart - thus scuppering his future earning potential. A 'tomato can' - to use the American term - is a hired fall guy who will fold as soon as the going gets tough. Unfortunately for us, Arturs Geikins didn't fit into either category. Only 4 fights into his paid career, he still had a winning fighter's ego and the punching power to go with it. He was a dangerous man who had only found himself on the right hand side of the bill because he couldn't sell a ticket. Frank, on the other hand, was a good ticket seller as the ubiquitous 'Team Monkhouse' T-Shirts in the York Hall balcony attested. Those ensconced would have the best view in the house of an impending disaster

Frank seemed to have the edge in a lively opening round before walking on to a huge right hand in the next session and crashing heavily to the canvas. When he arose on jelly legs, I already had the towel cocked but waited until my man was mercilessly hammered on the ropes before hurling it across the ring as the referee intervened simultaneously. Having scored his second win in 5 starts, Geikins felt entitled to celebrate with an exultant display of primordial chest beating, which was forgivable under the circumstances. In appropriate contrast, Frank was devastated and clearly held me at least partially responsible. A week later I got a text informing me that he was 'thinking of trying my luck with a new coach...' Predictably, I took umbrage and accused him of passing the buck but the simple truth is that he made the right call. I wasn't giving Frankie the entry level of commitment and professionalism that he - or any fighter - deserved. I was constantly late for sessions, perpetually hungover and wreaking of booze at the best of times. On the worst days, I wouldn't show up at all, having concocted some dubious excuse for my absence. Alec Wilkey, a veteran coach who also worked out of TKO took over the reins and got Frank a couple of wins before precisely the same thing happened against another Latvian banana skin. If I felt at all vindicated then it was purely out of reluctance to take responsibility for my own personal failings. Frankie Monkhouse was one of the good guys and I'm glad he got his hand raised one more time before hanging them up.

At the tail end of the year, Big Larry got his drugs ban commuted by virtue of singing like the illegitimate love child of Michael Buble and Maria Callas. Following a technical decision loss to

Sam Sexton in January 2012, he tested positive for EPO, the same stimulant that is thought to have propelled Lance Armstrong to 7 Tour De France titles prior to his disgrace. Initially, Larry protested his innocence and insisted on the costly B-sample analysis but when that came back dirty he held his hands up - not merely to the charge on the table but a further dozen banned substances that he suddenly remembered ingesting at one time or another.

Despite swearing he was clean since the Repton days, he later informed me that his introduction to EPO had occurred during a training stint at Freddie Roach's Wildcard Gym in Los Angeles. At the time Roach was working with a well known strength and conditioning guru whose name was synonymous with industry rumours of performance enhancing drugs and he had been the source, said Larry. The UK Anti - Doping Association duly meted out a 4 year ban but that punishment was more than cut in half when he agreed to give evidence against a Scottish super middleweight called Craig Windsor Jr. Curiously, Windsor Jr. hadn't failed a test and his conviction was based solely on a series of damning messages exchanged between he and Larry on Facebook concerning the availability and efficacy of various illegal steroids. How the messages came to UKAD's attention in the first place remains a mystery but Larry's willingness to expose them in return for his reinstatement is beyond dispute.

As soon as he got the green light to resume his career, Larry was offered a berth in the UK vs USA Heavyweight Prizefighter and approached me to train him for the tournament. Some suggested that it wouldn't look good for me to work with a proven drugs cheat who had only been reprieved at another fighter's expense but, from my perspective, our friendship superseded the peripheral negatives. From a selfish point of view there was also the allure of another moment in the spotlight and a chance to collect 10 percent of the grand prize money. The icing on the cake was the inclusion of James Toney, a bona fide all time great who was wringing the last drops of commercial value from his illustrious name. At 45, James was shot to bits and his diction was worryingly torpid but the possibility of facing hm in the opposite corner still held a certain magnitude.

When the fighters assembled the day before the weigh in for a Sky TV promo, Toney was surly and uncooperative in the extreme. He refused to take his shirt off for the photographs - perhaps due to a well documented proclivity for junk food that had made middleweight a distant memory - and generally behaved as if the whole carry on was insultingly beneath him. His unapproachability not withstanding, I kept my distance when he was in proximity on the grounds that any fannish behaviour would have been inappropriate. Later, when the principals had retired to their rooms in the Tower Hotel, a fire alarm went off leading some to surmise that the star of the show was in the throes of a characteristic mood swing

On the morning of the show, I saw Anthony Joshua - who would have his third pro fight on the card - eating breakfast with a friend in the downstairs restaurant. Although known to the British public for his Olympic success, his notoriety hadn't risen to a level that prevented him from moving around like a regular Joe at this point. Present in the flesh that night at York Hall was a special guest to whom Joshua and Toney paled in comparison. To give the occasion some extra gravitas, the legendary Larry Holmes had been flown in and seated ringside with his lovely wife, Diane, who cheerfully deferred to the hordes of selfie seeking fans that converged upon them. Janine was also in the house and I found it rather irksome that the 'Easton Assassin' seemed more interested in my lady and her black leather trousers than he was in my fawning superlatives. Allegedly, he invited her and a friend to meet for drinks afterwards although it's conceivable she was winding me up.

Back in the changing room, a middle aged man from UKAD scrutinised Larry's every move, as if he suspected that PEDS were taken in the same time frame as a pre fight snack. If the 'War Machine' was still on something, one hates to think how he might have performed unaided as he tripped over his own feet within 16 seconds and dropped a decision to Jason Gavern in the first quarter final. An affable redneck cop originally from Virginia, Gavern was possessed of modest skills and a low brow charisma that seemed to resonate with the crowd, especially his habit of yelling 'WOOOO' at various stages of the fight. Aside from the dubious knockdown, the highlight of the action came at the end of the first round when Larry landed a punch after the bell which drew an acrimonious response from his opponent. In the heat of the moment, I charged across the ring and pushed the American before referee, Richie Davies, chased me back to the corner and growled, "I AM IN CONTROL OF THIS FUCKING FIGHT, NOT YOU..!" My cameo was captured on TV, prompting Johnny Eames to remark, "YOU fought better then he did," when I saw him at TKO the following week.

Gavern went on to beat Toney in what constituted the upset of the night before losing to Michael Sprott in the final. By that time, Janine and I were already heading back to the hotel in a Matchroom company car, eager to make the most of a romantic evening by the riverside. If she had a genius, it was in making me feel as if every night we spent together was a first date with the shimmering promise of sexual reward. In past relationships I had become lackadaisical toward such things over time but, with Janine, it never got old. Something in her ambience suggested that no man could ever possess her entirely. It was maddening and exhilarating all at once.

After a few drinks in the bar and post -mortem banter with the melting pot of fighters, managers and camp aides, we retired to the room and ordered innumerable cocktails to fuel our corporeal intimacy. Somewhat at variance with the desired mood, Jason Gavern could be heard jabbering excitedly in the adjoining room, presumably on a mobile phone. Still high from his night's activity, he had evidently resolved to call every person of his acquaintance back home in order to bring them up to speed with his heroism. In fairness, if I had beaten James Toney at any point before his 70th birthday, I might have been a tad exuberant, too.

When we checked out the next morning, I was rather indignant to be confronted with an exorbitant bar tab and a polite but firm request for its prompt settlement.

On the day of the weigh in, I'd heard worrying noises that Matchroom were no longer willing to foot the bill for gratuitous indulgence and would only be paying for our bed and board. I was sufficiently concerned to take the matter up with long term 'Head of Boxing', John Wischhusen, who relented, "You can order wine with meals but don't go mad." Relieved at the concession, I took 'wine' to be a broad description for a wider range of alcoholic beverages and concluded that 'going mad' was open to interpretation.

"I've already cleared this with Johnny Wish," I insisted to the poor foreign lady on reception before whisking Janine through the revolving doors with an appropriate mixture of confidence and haste. Although I never heard another word about it, the seeds of my tenure in the official Matchroom bad books were probably sewn that day.

And things would only get worse.

17/ FISH EYES

"Hello..?"

The voice sounded unmistakably familiar but I couldn't place it.

"Hi, this is Ben Doughty returning a missed call."

"This is Frank Warren."

Although we had never spoken before, I instantly knew that it was Frank Warren and not some wag who fancied himself as an impressionist.

"What can I do for you, Frank..?"

"Right…You have uploaded a video to your YouTube channel that is potentially libellous and you need to take it down or you've got a problem. And…whilst we're on it…. That person sitting next to you in the video – who used to fight for about 5 grand – you need to ask yourself; what was he doing in 2004, in a car with several kilos of heroin…? And Alex Morrison needs to stop what he's doing because he has got another writ heading his way…."

Struggling to keep abreast of the relevance of his stream of invective, I interrupted:

"Frank… Honest to God, I have nothing against you. I'm admire your legacy in boxing."

"Erm…Well, ok," he muttered, seemingly disarmed by such flattery, "If you want a proper interview, pick up the phone and speak to me…!"

"I'd love to do an interview with you, Frank."

"Well delete that silly video and call me next week…!" he suggested before hanging up.

It was a Saturday morning in February, 2014 and I was playing with the kids in the park near their grandmother's house when

I noticed the missed call from an unrecognised number. The video to which Frank had irately referred was a 2 year old skit on 'Doughty and The Spirit' that focussed on a rare controversial book about Warren and his eventually acrimonious relationship former IBF light welterweight champion, Terry Marsh. In November,1989, Warren had been shot by a masked gunman outside the Broadway Theatre in Barking as he arrived for one of his promotions. A 9mm bullet from a Luger pistol missed his heart by an inch and he lost half a lung. Marsh was charged with the attempted murder and spent 10 months on remand before being acquitted in a show trial at the Old Bailey. Nobody else was ever charged in relation to the incident although Warren has claimed in recent years that he knows the identity of his would be assassin but refuses to be drawn further.

For my money, the YouTube video was harmless if rather puerile but, being possessed of a pathological sensitivity, Frank Warren was evidently not amused. He had sued the publishers of the book entitled 'Lords Of The Ring' and succeeded in having it pulped. My brandishing of one of the few surviving copies in a light hearted 'Whodunnit' sketch had obviously not gone down well. For me, the incident represented a 'Jim'll Fix It' moment. Frank Warren was a British boxing legend from the era of my childhood and here he was phoning ME to give a piece of his mind. That made me a 'face', I decided, and the ear bashing was a small price to pay for the confirmation. Eddie Hearn might be a charming and charismatic individual but the Frank Warren story was vastly more interesting from any historical perspective. He hadn't come from money or privilege, he came from the arse end of Islington and had clawed his way to the top with a ferocious business savvy allied to an obsessive need to rise above the competition. I couldn't think of too many 'non participants' I would rather talk to on camera than Uncle Frank.

Before that was deemed possible, press officer Richard Maynard insisted I publish an apology for my referencing of the evil book and the egregious slurs that it cast upon his virtuous employer. I did my best to pull if off without coming across as a blatantly grovelling wanker and figured I would delete the evidence as soon as my mission was accomplished. Maynard was apparently satisfied and invited me to attend a press conference at Frederick's restaurant in the Angel on February 13 where Mr. Warren would be available to answer my questions.

I turned up on the day accompanied by veteran cameraman Eric Guy who had offered his services for free in what amounted to a departure from normality. When we arrived at the exclusive brasserie in Camden Passage, a gentleman who happened to be Frank Warren's older brother was stood outside. I became aware of this genealogy on account of Eric's visible familiarity. "Hello Robert, you old bastard..! He's come to interview your brother." In the ensuing years, I would often bump into Robert on the circuit and found him a constantly cheerful presence in rather blatant contrast to his legendary sibling.

The purpose of the presser itself was to give a final plug to a double header at the Copper Box Arena featuring Tyson Fury and Dereck Chisora in co main events. Del Boy was pitted against the perennial gatekeeper, Kevin Johnson, whilst Fury had a less demanding assignment vs one Joey Abell, who was arguably oversold by his nomenclature. Eric and I took our seats and witnessed a rather forgettable affair that failed to produce any arresting sound-bytes, despite the 'Gypsy King's presence which ordinarily guaranteed such things. It was clear that the whole press conference ritual had changed in the YouTube era, with everyone playing it close to the chest and waiting on their clickbait exclusives. When the fighters moved away from the dais to accommodate the various requests for 1-2-1s, I walked over to Warren and introduced myself. He shook my hand warmly, as if I might be a long lost pal, and offered, "Alright, mate. How are you…?" Unremarkable though it reads in print, it was literally as if someone had turned on a charm switch located at back of his neck. He was impeccably dressed, as always, in a conservative dark blue suit and polka dot blue tie. Feeling that it was 'a bit chilly' to conduct an interview in the garden, he suggested we set up at a table near the window.

Before we started rolling, I assured the naturally suspicious kingpin that I had no interest in 'scandal mongering' or petty controversy. The assertion was intended to put him at ease but it happened to be true. And neither could I give a toss about Fury or Chisora and their run of the mill engagements 2 nights hence. I had come for the real Frank Warren story from Canonbury to Canastota, with no stone left unturned.

"I didn't even set out to be a boxing promoter, really," he started to explain. "Some things happen by accident.. I got involved, I got bitten by the bug as a lot of people do in boxing and, from there, I strived to do the best I could. Whatever I get involved with, I always try to make sure it's the best."

After cutting his teeth in the seedy underbelly of the so called unlicensed scene, Frank had entered the more legitimised game at the tail end of 1980, when the fabled 'Cartel' had a stranglehold on British Boxing in terms of television and major venues. The Board of Control that he would practically own one day had conspired with the powers that were in a further effort to freeze him out.

"Everywhere I went, I was getting the door shut in my face and I wasn't prepared to allow that to happen from my perspective," he recounted.

When the conversation turned to 'fractious relationships' with fighters great and good, I seized my opportunity to mention the name that few dared to utter in his presence.

"Everybody who follows boxing knows that your first world champion was Terry Marsh…"

His neck twitched in that habitual mannerism that seemed to suggest vulnerability and defiance in equal measure and he just about nodded. Where was I going with this...? I hadn't thought it through and was suddenly groping for the most innocuous question in the context of Terry Marsh that I could think of. Did he recognise Terry's world class potential at the outset...? It was weak and, inevitably, Frank smashed it out of the park.

"I'm very short and sweet on that. He won a world title under ME. Defended it in his hometown, under my promotion. I put the money up, that happened and I don't want to talk anymore about Terry Marsh."

One former friend turned foe that he did wish to talk about was Alex Morrison. An old school Glasgow face with a fearsome reputation north of the border, Morrison had been very vocal in alleging that his fighter, Ricky Burns, was still owed a substantial amount of money for his most recent world title defence under Frank's promotion. Whether such claims were founded or not, Burns had severed the alliance and signed with Matchroom, as had other big names formerly contracted to Warren, including Kell Brook and Tony Bellew. As well as refuting the accusations of non payment, Frank was contesting the legality of Burns' defection. Clearly hacked off with Morrison's constant barbs on social media, our hero sought to close the interview with a vitriolic trashing of his online nemesis.

"Let's talk about Alex Morrison. I won a libel action against him 2 weeks ago. The damages and costs are being assessed and he will have to pay them. Or, if he doesn't pay them, I'll bankrupt him, simple as that. Where is the contract he refers to..? Why hasn't anybody asked him WHERE is this contract that he keeps referring to..? Where would Alex Morrison have been without me...?"

Suddenly he plucked a phone from his trouser pocket and exhibited a screen shot of a recent call from Morrison, alleging that the latter had been "Crying on my telephone....trying to get himself of the hook…. Now he's a woman scorned… He's had his arse kicked in court because he lied….. and all he's doing now is digging a bigger and bigger hole."

As he reached a crescendo of righteous indignation, it was impossible to be wholly unimpressed with this tenacious old bastard who had survived bullets, bankruptcy and battery only to bounce back stronger on each occasion. Oddly, he didn't actually realise that I was the same person whom he had torn a strip off several days earlier until I alluded to our previous conversation. Perhaps that's why he had been so convivial at the outset. Certainly, it was the last time he would show me such bonhomie.

The 25 minute interview was well received in boxing circles, with one predictable exception. Within hours of the upload going live, I got a message from Alex Morrison's daughter requesting a right to reply on her father's behalf. She stressed that they had no axe to grind in terms of my professional conduct and simply desired an opportunity to redress the balance. Somewhat excited to be on the radar of such people but wary of being caught in a crossfire, I agreed to talk to 'Big Alex' at my next convenience with the caveat that I wouldn't travel to Scotland for that express purpose. She understood and we made a loose agreement that if my business found me in Glasgow anytime soon then a meeting would be arranged.

6 months later, my business did find me in Glasgow. After losing to Gavern, Big Larry opted to go on the road and lost 3 fights on the spin, including a particularly embarrassing first round stoppage defeat at the hands of former super middleweight, Jamie Hearn. In what would almost certainly prove to be a case of '4th time unlucky' he was brought in as an opponent for the up and coming Scottish heavyweight, Garry Cornish, in an 8 round main event at the Paisley Lagoon Centre. Holed up in a modest motel on the outskirts of the city, on the afternoon of the fight I took a taxi to Morrison's Gym in Glasgow's East End. I arrived to find it empty save for a lone shadow boxer in the ring and

the proprietor seated at a hefty oak desk in the office at the rear of the building. He was an imposing figure of a man, around 17 stone, with distinguished white hair and a rugged countenance that betrayed a chequered past. Despite the overtones of gangsterism associated with this name, he could probably have passed for a grizzled academic had a director seen fit to cast him in the role. Bizarrely, he opened with, "I thought you might be a black guy…" Assuming he had actually seen the Warren interview, one could only wonder about the colour settings of the device on which he had chosen to view it.

I took a seat on the other side of the desk and started filming on my phone, kicking off with a sprinkling of harmless questions about the early days. At 43, he had been the oldest man in history to win the Scottish Western District title as an amateur heavyweight before making his name on the safer and often more lucrative side of the ropes. It hadn't always been lucrative, he admitted with a wry smile as he recalled Mickey Duff's favourite line when counting the spoils from their various co promotions.

"He would say, 'Alex, the operation was a success. But I'm afraid the patient died.'" He chuckled and added that Mickey was good company but 'so tight that he squeaked when he walked.' In the summer of 2000, he had played host to Mike Tyson ahead of his fight with Lou Savarese at Hampden Park. Iron Mike was 'Ok' he remembered despite being more committed to 'smoking ganja in the toilet' than he was to the rigours of training. He related a story of the iconic puncher Koing a pair of unfortunate sparring partners in double quick time before returning to his preferred recreation. In 1974, he had met Muhammad Ali before the Frazier rematch and – according to the tale – upon hearing a Scottish accent, The Greatest had quipped, "You came all this way to watch 2 Niggas fight…?"

In due course, I cut to the chase and Mr. Morrison reiterated his claim that Ricky Burns was still owed a 6 figure sum for his fight with Kevin Mitchell in September, 2012. "We've had 3 or 4 bouncing checks and promise after promise," he sighed gravely. "I'm speaking up for Ricky because he's a quiet person. It's a shame I had to fall out with Frank because we had some good times."

Considering it an appropriate denouement, I turned off the camera and my host asked if I wanted something to eat. Not wishing to spurn his hospitality, we got into a grey Range Rover parked outside and drove to his detached home in an affluent looking suburb about 20 minutes away. I was introduced to Mrs. Morrison and, after proudly showing me his makeshift gym at the bottom of the garden, he called a taxi to take the 3 of us to an Italian Restaurant in Princes Square shopping centre. The anecdotes continued and the red wine flowed. Ordinarily, it would have been unprofessional to get half sloshed before cornering a professional prize fighter but I saw it as a case of horses for courses. Seeing as Larry had no intention of trying to win, as long as I wasn't sufficiently insensible that I'd forgotten how to rinse a gum shield then my blood alcohol concentration levels were unlikely to make a difference. And in fairness, it took an awful lot of booze before my motor skills and eloquence were noticeably affected.

A few hours later, Larry lost every round whist turning in a performance that might have qualified for a Nobel Peace Prize nomination had it not been so stultifyingly hard to watch. Cornish didn't seem up to much either but at least he was familiar with the concept of aiming a clenched fist in his opponent's direction. Whatever it was that had briefly made Larry a destroyer of men was clearly not there anymore and people are welcome to form their own conclusions as to where it might have gone. Fighters like Peter Buckley or Johnny Greaves knew how to lose in style and provide a bit of theatre but this was a cynical exercise that ultimately served as much purpose as a condom in a nunnery. On the plus side, it was easy money and got me out and about on the scene.

It also paid for the drinks as I mingled in the motel bar until 2am before catching 3 hours sleep and taking a taxi to the airport. I insisted on an early flight back to London as I had things to do that Sunday, including a Muhammad Ali film premiere in Whitechapel with special guests like John Conteh and Herol Graham. I knew that the Morrison interview would ruffle a few feathers but failed to anticipate the extent of the fallout and the enduring problems it would create for me in an industry full of thin skinned sociopaths and simpering lackeys. At the end of the day, whatever had gone on between Messrs Warren, Burns and Morrison was their business and I should have kept well out of it.

18/ VIVA LAS VEGAS

We were preparing for take-off when I received the email from Hill Dickinson, the law firm that represented Frank Warren. Already several glasses of Champagne to the good, I briefly skimmed its rather long winded content before exclaiming, "Hey fellas', I think Frank Warren might be suing me…!"
The attached letter was signed by one Kevin Carpenter and alluded to 'pre action protocol for defamation' and various other things that sounded quite serious and foreboding. Although the legal threats and complex terminology were intended to intimidate, this latest development merely fed into my sky rocketing ego and sense of importance. Before losing signal, I took a degree of pleasure in curtly responding, 'I am currently en route to Las Vegas but will deal with this matter upon my return to the UK next week.' I wasn't sure if the communication represented an attempt to scare me or if it might have graver implications but, either way, it could wait.

It was the morning of September 11, 2014 and five of us were heading to Sin City for the Floyd Mayweather - Marcos Maidana rematch taking place at the MGM Grand Garden in two days time. In view of my haphazard approach to bookkeeping, it was a minor miracle that the trip was coming to fruition at all. Having decided that my social media trajectory had reached a point at which I could broker big fight packages, I had advertised the jaunt several weeks earlier on Facebook, setting the price at £1425 per head. In retrospect, it would be fair to say that I wasn't acutely aware of what I was doing and had plucked that figure out of the air. Neil from Liverpool was the first to transfer the cold hard cash to my bank account, closely followed by Shane, a multi millionaire property developer who paid for his own berth plus that of a trusted employee in lieu of his annual bonus.

Suddenly, I had 4 thousand, two hundred and seventy five pounds off the back of a Facebook post. Embarrassing admission though it may be, it was the largest sum of money I'd ever had to my name at any particular time. If you have paid attention up to now then my disclosure should hardly come as a shocking revelation, admittedly. Assuming there would be some kind of profit margin involved, I celebrated that evening with a few drinks in the Durham Arms, a throwback East London boozer about 5 minutes walk from TKO Gym. Although the money wasn't mine, the mere fact that it was in my possession engendered a bogus sense of solvency that I found quite agreeable. The realisation that I had amassed sufficient credibility for relative strangers to throw sizeable sums of money in my direction was the worst thing that could have happened to an alcoholic and Vegas would be the turning point.

The next day I purchased 8 tickets for the fight via the Golden Boy website and contacted a travel agent in Manchester, looking for cheap flights and a decent hotel near The Strip. Knowing that I would need a few more customers to make it work, it was of crucial importance what I could pay in increments and had the option of adding more passengers at a later date. After due consideration, I plumped for indirect flights with Virgin and 3 nights in the Riviera with the full balance to be paid 3 weeks before the departure date. Any failure to do so on my part would result in the forfeiture of the total deposit.

In order to cover my own flights and accommodation, I needed at least half a dozen punters but, hereafter, only one more was forthcoming. To cut a long story short, the fight tickets cost twice as much as I anticipated which - combined with the lack of sales - left me 3 thousand pounds shy of the target. Standing to lose everyone's money and fearing the ruin of my good name, late August was characterised by sleepless nights as my mind raced through every conceivable option for averting disaster. Coincidentally, I was reading Nick Leeson's 'Rogue Trader' at the time and saw myself in tandem with the book's protagonist, despite the chicken feed nature of my financial burden in comparison.

With only days until the deadline, I decided that Facebook had

THROWING IN THE TOWEL

got me into this mess and so Facebook would have to bust me out. Accordingly, I put out a status that calmly contended: 'I need a small amount of investment for a lucrative boxing project. Interested parties please inbox me.' Within an hour, I was inundated with enquiries from potential investors - one of whom, ironically, was 'Millionaire Shane.' Although I didn't relish admitting that I needed the 3k to salvage a trip that he had already paid for, instinctively I knew he was the most serious of the bunch. It was a Sunday afternoon when he called and I explained that costs had risen due to circumstances beyond my control but if he was willing to put up the additional money then perhaps I could make him a partner in the business. With the casual air of a man throwing pocket change to a derelict, he replied, "Ok, I'll put the money across in an hour, when I get home." Allowing my shoulders to relax for the first time in a fortnight, I thanked him profusely before hanging up. The relief was almost tangible but a vicious circle was being created in which Facebook became my go to resource to extricate myself from whatever financial hole I might have dug myself into. It was always going to end in tears.

We had a 3 hour stopover in LA before our connecting flight landed in Las Vegas at 8pm local time. According to our British body clocks, it was 4am in the morning and most of us had been drinking steadily since breakfast time. In addition to my friend, Jim - a former PT client who had recently come out of the closet - the entourage now included an old mate of Neil's, who also hailed from Liverpool but lived in North Carolina for whatever reason. He went halves with Neil on the room and bought one of the 3 spare tickets in my possession which put some urgently needed spending money in my pocket. The plan was coming together.

Running on adrenaline and boyish camaraderie, we took a limo from the airport to the hotel and arranged to reconvene in the lobby after a cursory shower and change. Ablutions having been performed, Shane proposed an excursion Downtown and a pair of taxis were commandeered at around 10pm Opting to ride with Shane and his confederate, I left Jim to pile in with the Scousers although it occurred to me that they might not be the most gay friendly of travel companions. At variance with the plan, our drivers lost each other at the first set of lights and so Shane, Tim and I wound up in a joint called the Commonwealth on Fremont Street, without the other three. Having been so easily separated on our first night in the storied Mecca of chance, inevitable quips were made alluding to the plot of 'The Hangover' but there were no blackouts or impromptu marriages at our end. The 2am cab ride back to the Riviera was augmented by an interesting narration from our lady driver who drew our attention to the notorious 'Heart Attack Grill' before explaining that she used to be a topless dancer and struggled to find a man who wasn't invasively possessive. You had to feel for her.

Jim - my designated roommate - came back at 7am, relating his night's adventure with the comical urgency of a man clearly fuelled by something more than nature's amphetamines. He had ditched the Scousers early doors and made the acquaintance of a 'Black Mexican' drug dealer who was peddling cocaine on a 'try before you buy' basis. The coke was off the charts said Jim but when he attempted to withdraw some cash from the nearest ATM, he was dismayed to find that no American tender was forthcoming. Regarding an attempted transaction in Nevada as suspicious, Barclays had frozen his account pending confirmation but what did the 'Blaxican' know about UK banking protocols…? Unwilling to admit defeat, Jim got into the man's SUV as they proceeded to hit every cash machine within a 2 mile radius, hoping for a different result. Way off the beaten track, he suddenly began to fear for his safety and asked, "Are you going to hurt me…?" The Blaxican calmly chopped out some more lines on the dashboard before handing him a rolled up bill and drawling. "We cool, just hook me up tomorrow, Dog." For a man who made his living on the fringes of the pharmaceutical industry he sounded very easy going by Jim's excitable account.

After meeting up for brunch at Denny's, the retinue made its way to the weigh in which was being held in the MGM. Riddick Bowe was the first big name we spotted amongst the teeming crowds but when I requested a picture he growled, "No, how much money you got…?" I'd heard the rumblings that 'Big Daddy' had fallen on hard times and his behaviour seemed entirely consistent with that. Once the Undisputed Heavyweight Champion of the World, his relegation to the status of 'has been' must have been hard to stomach, especially when Floyd 'Money' Mayweather was commanding 'telephone numbers' every time he stepped into the ring. From my standpoint, his rejection was survivable.

The modern big fight weigh in has become an increasingly drawn out procedure, attended by hundreds or even thousands of fans who may or may not go to the fight itself. We were largely bored throughout the unreasonably long performance of a Latino pop star, unknown to us but evidently appreciated by a gaggle of screaming young Hispanic girls in our midst. Thankfully, the anodyne warbler was eventually replaced by the gangsta rap of Rick Ross and the teenage girls were suddenly superseded by Afro American males making obligatory hand gestures as free T - Shirts bearing the TBE logo were shot into the crowd from bizarre hand held cannons. Surrounded by such extravagant frippery, I couldn't help but contrast it with the era in which Joe Louis and Jack Sharkey would smile wanly and shake hands before heading off to eat a steak.

Peckish and underwhelmed, we left early in search of similar sustenance. My friend and future southern area champion, Ben Day, was in town with his long suffering girlfriend, Nerice, and so we met up for lunch at the Rainforest Cafe. Although they hadn't come for the fight specifically, Ben decided to take the remaining tickets off my hands which gave me another few hundred dollars to play with. At least I wasn't going to run out of beer money. Gambling wasn't my thing so there was no chance of me squandering it at the tables, unlike Neil who seemed to do little else and had already taken a kicking at the hands of the croupiers.

Before we left, I got a call from 'Iceman' John Scully, a former light heavyweight contender turned trainer, inviting us to the grand opening of the new Rival store on East Sunset Rd near the airport. It would be a star studded affair, with Roy Jones and Lennox Lewis both expected alongside a whole host of 80s and 90s boxing celebrities. I was also looking forward to meeting Scully with whom I'd forged a kinship over the years on Facebook. He was an inscrutable boxing man who shared my passionate views on the egregious nature of the sanctioning bodies and their relentless bastardisation of our once great sport.

A few hours later, we arrived in a garish 'party bus' bedecked with disco lights and a lap dancer's pole. We weren't being deliberately ostentatious and had merely been advised that it was the cheapest mode of transportation for a party of eight. Nevertheless, it did rather create the impression of Brits on the piss, gate crashing a haven of boxing royalty. Russ Anber was the man behind the Rival brand and opening a store in Las Vegas was the realisation of 'a life long dream' he explained when the time came for speeches. Having worked with numerous elite fighters, he was basically Canada's Mr. Boxing and very well liked in the industry. That much was apparent from the sheer volume of faces who had turned out to raise a glass to his new venture. Food and booze was laid on but I was starting to feel fragile and resolved to give my constitution a rest for a couple of hours.

Lennox Lewis was in the house as advertised but seemed preoccupied and aloof. For such a great fighter his aura was hardly incandescent, I noted. Suddenly, Neil spotted Sugar Ray Leonard chatting to Roy Jones Jr and quickly drew my attention to the priceless cameo of twin icons in quiet conference. In accordance with the dress down code, Sugar Ray wore an open neck black shirt while Pensacola's favourite son sported a navy blue polo shirt with white stripes. This was one exclusive gathering and no mistake. I asked Ray if he remembered our interview 2 years ago in London and he made out as if he did although I suspect he was just being nice. Thanks to John Scully who put in a good word for 'one of the top boxing guys in England,' Roy consented to an exclusive Q and A in the parking lot.

He was on his last legs as an active prizefighter but still looked a million dollars with ridiculously bulging biceps that would not have appeared incongruous on a Marvel superhero. With Scouse Neil acting as an impromptu cameraman, we plotted outside in the cool night air as the constant noise of transiting aircrafts threatened to drown the audio. I asked him about the bittersweet nature of being named the outstanding boxer of Seoul '88 despite that notorious robbery in the final.

"There were TWO truths," he replied. "I was the gold medal winner and I was the best boxer of the games. They just gave me half of the truth."

The highlights of his glorious hey day were covered before I alluded to the radical decline after his celebrated win over John Ruiz in 2003. His physical genius had been second to none but Roy was clearly no historian. He had dropped back down to light heavyweight , he explained, in order to replicate the heroics of Bob Fitzsimmons at the turn of the century.
I pointed out that 'Ruby Robert' had actually captured the 175 pound laurels in 1903 having already reigned as middle and heavyweight king.

"No..!" he insisted. "He won the middleweight, light heavyweight and heavyweight. Then he went back and recaptured the light heavyweight...."

"Roy, I swear to God he did it a different order. He won the heavyweight title in 1897 and beat George Gardner for the almost inaugural light heavyweight title AFTER that fact." He had to be wrong because the light heavyweight division wasn't heard of until 1903.

Sensing that the waters had gotten a little deep, he shrugged, "Ok, well if I'd have known that, I wouldn't have had to lose that weight…!"

At this point, it occurred to me that the audacious gamble was playing out rather well. I had pitched on the basis that I was a man with connections in high places and, on this evidence, nobody was about to call me a liar. We thanked Roy for his time just as Sugar Ray Leonard was pulling away in his Tahoe Hybrid and the undefeated heavyweight, Deontay Wilder, strolled past in a gaudy cyber yellow ensemble. The 'Bronze Bomber' was on the verge of a WBC title shot but in context he was a can of John West pink salmon surrounded by swordfish and caviar. Even his towering frame and luminous dress sense couldn't excavate him from the shadow of greatness.

In the interests of frugality, we left in the same motorised monstrosity we had arrived in, asking the driver to stop at the MGM. On the eve of a big fight, the action revolved around the Lobby Bar - through which anybody who was anybody seemed to pass as if it were a contracted obligation. Also prevalent were the scores of high end escorts mingling with the crowd in search of business. Having pulled off another journalistic coup, I was now drinking with a vengeance as was Ben Day with whom I spent much of the night clinking glass as he continually shouted "ROY JONES…!"

Familiar fellow Brits included Spencer - resplendent in waistcoat, shirt and tie - Matt Christie from Boxing News and veteran broadsheet correspondent, Kevin Mitchell who bolstered my ego when he said, "You and Kugan are showing a new path." In truth, I had nowhere near Kugan's traction but the sentence had a pleasant ring to it, all the same. As we sat on high stools at the bar, a gorgeous young black hooker asked if she could join us and proceeded to waste at least an hour of her life setting me up for the kill. When she eventually asked, "So what are your plans for the night..?" I yawned and replied, "I think I'll go to bed shortly. Big day tomorrow."

"Do you want any company…?"

"No," I said simply. I wanted to say something more charming and apologetic but that was all that came out. I wouldn't have cheated on Janine for free, never mind whatever exorbitant rate at which this Chocolate Aphrodite was peddling her arse. I had a rum and coke for the road and took a cab back to the hotel, alone.

19/ STARSTRUCK

When Mike Tyson entered the Las Vegas Convention Centre, nobody could escape the shade of an aura that seemed to trample everything in its wake. Not Roy Jones nor Riddick Bowe, nor Earnie Shavers, Leon Spinks, Zab Judah, Sergio Martinez or anyone else amongst the impressive array of fistic dignitaries on hand. Not even the naked Latino chick, daubed in body paint for some kind of automobile promotion could compete with the head turning magnetism of the main man and the impossibly durable fascination with his every deed and diatribe. The world seemed to spin more slowly on its axis as he traipsed into my vicinity and randomly proffered his hand. He was wearing light blue slacks and a white V – neck T Shirt from which hung a laminate, in case anybody didn't know that he was Mike Tyson. As with Sugar Ray almost 10 years earlier, I refused to let go of the hand as I began, "I can't imagine my teenage years without YOU. I even lost my virginity on the day you knocked out Berbick." "That's cool," he offered before talking his seat at a table beside which a long queue was forming.

Suddenly, Spencer appeared out of nowhere looking for all the world as if Tinie Tempah had infiltrated an exclusive lawn tennis club. It wasn't every man who could pull off white canvas shorts and a Ralph Lauren sweater with bow tie and purple lenses. He was holding a cordless microphone and evidently acting as a master of ceremonies although how his appointment came about was anybody's guess. Joining the fabled former heavyweight king at the table were 3 young prospects signed to the recently formed 'Iron Mike Productions', one of them a Hispanic welterweight with the same facial tattoo as his hero. Behind the table was a 10 ft square show ring and when the Hispanic kid moved, I attempted to sneak through the ropes and claim the empty chair on Tyson's left. Security were quick to pounce before Spencer bellowed into the mic, "LEAVE HIM ALONE, HE'S ONE OF MY BEST FRIENDS FROM LONDON..!"

The bouncers backed off and allowed me to take the most coveted seat in the building as Spencer continued to hold court with his stream of Afro – Cockney consciousness. My new best friend seemed half sedated – presumably on account of whatever psychotropic drugs he was taking – but he was a good listener. I talked and he nodded with unmistakable sensitivity for what might have been a period of 5 minutes. Despite his abject lack of verbiage, it was a profound emotional experience for which I wasn't fully prepared. Even mute, he had a gargantuan presence that Lennox Lewis could only have dreamt about. Those who were fortunate enough to make his acquaintance say that Muhammad Ali had it, too.

Not wishing to wear out my welcome, I shook the hand once more and got up to leave. Before doing so, I was euphoric enough to transgress the regular boundaries of our friendship and give Spencer a hug.
Gathering up the rest of the gang, I insisted we leave at once and go in search of an agreeable spot for lunch. I had no interest in the anti climax of engaging with other guests at the inaugural Boxing Fan Expo and had the big fight been cancelled due to a bomb scare – at that moment – I couldn't have cared less.

When we were escorted to our seats in the MGM Grand later that night, I struggled to comprehend the pricing bands that had forced me to shell out $600 per head, thus causing the initial budgeting crisis. So far as I could tell, we were in the uppermost 'Gods' so how our positioning represented an upgrade from the $300 options was a mystery. Because I had purchased our tickets via 2 separate transactions, I sat with Ben and Nerice while the rest of the lads watched in a noisy pro Maidana section that left Shane convinced that 'Chino' had been robbed. In fairness, he was way off beam as Mayweather cruised to a unanimous decision over an adversary who had given him a sterner tussle in the same building 4 months earlier.

Aside from the minor drama of a right hand that stiffened the WBC welterweight champion's legs at the end of the third, it was reasonably plain sailing for the Michigan prodigy who incurred the ire of a booing crowd in the 12th and final round by virtue of his fleet footed refusal to engage. Profane though they were, one could sympathise with the mug punter's frustration. It's impossible to be a lover of the Sweet Science without acknowledging Floyd's contribution but it was a minimalist form of brilliance, quite devoid of the showmanship and charisma that marked the performances of Ali and Leonard in their pomp. Unquestionably, he was an artist but one could hardly call him an entertainer – at least not within the confines of the ropes.

If the fight didn't exactly set pulses racing then our exit from the venue certainly provided some spontaneous excitement as we were caught in a vaguely frightening stampede. I'd never seen American crowd violence before and wondered what could have happened to cause such a melee as people jostled, screamed and hollered in a concerted effort to squeeze through the gates. Amid varying rumours that somebody had been shot or a bomb had been found, Jim and I evacuated through a fire escape, having been separated from the others. Subsequently, there were no reports of any major incident or attendant casualties and, thanks to Wi-Fi, we were soon reunited and back on the piss in the New York – New York Casino. Unsure of how much longer my system could tolerate the consecutive stag night style benders, I suggested 'a quiet one' which duly translated into a raucous, tequila soaked shindig at Coyote Ugly until throwing out time at 4am. Shane, in particular, was of the opinion it had been 'an amazing few days' which was something of a relief, considering his crucial role in the venture. Somehow, I had pulled it off and gotten away with it.

The next morning we bumped into Kugan Cassius at the airport and I couldn't help but detect a trace of piety in his tone when he asked, "Are you DRUNK..?"
I had been on the Stellar Artois since 9am but didn't readily see what it had to do with him. Perhaps he had become perman-

ently locked in interviewer mode. When we landed at Gatwick on Monday September 15, it was time for me to face the music with Uncle Frank and his lawyers. In the interim, I had received a further email accusing me of a 'brazen attempt to hide the interview from our attention' – by allowing it to be posted on a 3rd party channel – with the inference that 'you have been entirely reckless to the truth of the allegations.' In conclusion, I was invited to broadcast an apology along with a written explanation of my conduct and 'your proposals tor compensating our client in lieu of damages.'

Back in Canning Town, Jimmy Tibbs reckoned I had nothing to worry about as, in his words, "You ain't got any money have ya'…?" Agreeing that I was unlikely to crack the next Forbes Magazine listings, I reminded him that I still got about for a man of slender means. Without entering into any further correspondence, I told the 3rd party to delete the Alex Morrison interview and hoped it would be enough to get Hill Dickinson off my back. Ultimately, there were no legal repercussions but the episode did succeed in earning me the undying enmity of Mr. Warren who swore never to grant me another interview and has thus far kept his promise.

By Christmas, I was living in a threadbare single room above the Durham Arms as my relationship with Janine died a slow death. There were was no dramatic break up, just a gradual distancing on her part as she became increasingly disillusioned with my drinking and behaviours. I missed her savagely and was beginning to hate myself and the ever shrinking world that I inhabited. For years, I had gotten away with burning the candle at both ends but by now the corrugated 'abs' had given way to the ballooning gut of the habitual boozer. Chronically vain and in denial, I formed an aversion to sitting down as it accentuated the ghastly paunch. Consequently, when not downstairs in the bar, I would stand bolt upright in my dinghy room, knocking back hard liquor and tending to the Facebook flock until I passed out. Social media had created an impression of success and good standing but behind the façade was a lonely alcoholic who was now literally incapable of sitting with himself.

20/ MONTE CARLO OR BUST

There is nothing wrong with taking a glass of champagne at 5 O' Clock in the morning if one has the good fortune to be a temperate drinker. When travelling for the purpose of leisure, it was evidently part of Shane's pre flight routine to wash down a seafood platter with a half bottle of Dom Perignon courtesy of Caviar House and Prunier. At no point did this ritual appear to set him on the slippery slope and most of the lads were following his lead without guilt or shame. The party was 11 strong as we waited to board the 7.25am from Gatwick to Nice - en route to Monte Carlo in order to watch Martin Murray's unenviable bid to unseat Gennady Golovkin as the true Middleweight Champion of the World. "It's going to get messy," predicted former light middleweight prospect, George Hillyard. Unfortunately, things had already gotten messy for me a very long time ago and new depths awaited.

Immediately prior to this latest exotic sojourn, I had been sharing a house in Leytonstone with Jon and one of his platonic female friends. Not 2 weeks into the arrangement, my copybook was blotted when I helped myself to a bottle of sparkling rose, having risen in the small hours seeking liquid ease and comfort. Although Kaz worked in the field of addiction, she wasn't inclined to deal with such things outside of office hours and gave me a week's grace to find somewhere else to live. For the next 2 nights, I would be staying in one of Monaco's finest hotels but genuinely had no idea where I might be headed upon our return.

Once again, the trip was only happening due to the urgent philanthropy of a friend. This time, I had the hotels and flights covered but no tickets for the fight itself until Mick came to the rescue. The Salle des Etoiles was an exclusive venue that seated no more than a thousand spectators. In view of such a limited capacity, it was absurdly presumptuous of me to accept payments before I had even established the availability of fight tickets, never mind their likely inflated price. They turned out to be £500 a pop which meant that my total package price of £975 was about as realistic as a 1960s dinosaur flick.

As ever, I began to clutch at straws, putting my faith in a guy called William who promised to get me 10 tickets at £200 each plus a press accreditation for yours truly. William cut an incongruous figure on the London boxing scene due to a voluminous beard of which ZZ Top would not have been ashamed, juxtaposed with the superficial charm of the upper middle classes. He was the original blagger who talked a good game but was often found wanting when it came to the crunch. Briefly, he had positioned himself as the commercial agent of the popular super middleweight, Frank Buglioni, before the relationship evidently cooled. He also claimed to be tight with Golovkin and in my desperation to believe him, I paid a £500 deposit on what we had agreed. By the first week of February, William seemed to have gone AWOL and I became increasingly sceptical that he would honour the deal. It was time for Plan B.

When it came to the healthy state of his financial affairs, Mick threw people off the scent due to his excessively humble demeanour and passionate socialism. Like myself, he was an ex amateur boxer turned coach and also a recovering alcoholic who could spot the illness in me from a mile away. In deference to those points of affinity, he bailed me out with the 2 grand I needed to purchase the 11 tickets I had since managed to source through a more reliable, clean shaven contact. Once again, I had pulled it out of the fire but was getting far too accustomed to juggling other people's money and pledging to pay it back. Inexorably, I was heading toward rock bottom.

We landed in Nice at 10.30am and proceeded to Monte Carlo in a fleet of taxis. Initially, the travel agent had suggested we go by Helicopter for a small price increase but Shane was having none of that. It was a shame since a helicopter ride might have provided the perfect analogy for my modus operandi, being expensively flamboyant with the ever present fear of impending doom. There were further complications when we checked in at the Meridian Beach Plaza and the man on reception insisted that one of our rooms had not been paid for. It ought to have been my responsibility but the gentleman in question coughed up the difference out of his own pocket. In contrast to the Vegas trip, I was on a very tight budget and didn't have money to be throwing around. Unfortunately, I soon discovered that the Meridian was an unforgiving environment for the financially embarrassed. A club sandwich at the bar came to the equivalent of £27 and even a humble pint of lager cost the best part of a tenner. In dire need of the money that William still owed me, I briefed the group accordingly: "If anyone sees a bloke that looks like Jesus at a Hell's Angels convention then you must alert me immediately."

The weigh in at Casino de Monte Carlo was a dignified affair, devoid of the silly posturing and shoving that had long since become de rigueur. It wasn't in either fighter's nature to disrespect his opponent and - with the possible exception of Griffith - Paret - the juvenile insults never made a difference when the bell rang. Golovkin was the epitome of a sophisticated Bond villain who did his talking with his fists vs the tattooed lad from St. Helens who had used the noble art to escape a life of petty delinquency. Interestingly, Martin had won the ABA title at welterweight in the same tournament that had seen me lose to Jamie Morrison a decade earlier. If he could somehow conquer the formidable Kazak- already mooted as an all time great - it would certainly constitute a fairy tale.

Still smarting from the Leytonstone affair, I made the spurious sacrifice of abstaining from wine during a communal lunch at the Cafe De Paris. Beginning to identify alcohol as the chief cause of my numerous problems, I had good intentions of remaining dry for the weekend but, by nightfall, my resolve had dwindled. We were strolling along the marina looking for a suitable place to have dinner when 2 men who were also in town for the fight approached us with brazen familiarity. "Haven't you heard, lads...? The fight's off," said the larger one of the two who had a shaved head and an Irish accent. For an encore, he looked at me and observed, "You could be my twin... Only you're my ugly twin..!" His accomplice was around 5ft 8 with dark hair and turned about to be former professional boxer, Michael Graydon. They were looking for some action and one could sense the vague aura of trouble in their collective ambience. Whatever happened that night, it seems safe to assume that Adrian and Michael found more action than they could handle as the latter went missing and was eventually found dead at the bottom of a ravine. As obnoxious as the big guy was, I wish we had invited them to stay in our company.

On the morning of the fight, Murray's team held an impromptu press conference style gathering for the British fans staying in the hotel. Essentially, he was under no illusions as to the enormity of the task and had come to do his best. When somebody asked what he had made of Golovkin's most recent performance - against Marco Antonio Rubio - he replied, "I don't like watchin' boxin', mate. I 'ate it. I'd rather watch Peppa Pig with me kids." His response provided humour and light relief but there was nothing funny about the prospect of sharing a ring with Gennady Golovkin. He was going to need every modicum of encouragement that the 200 strong horde who called themselves 'Martin Murray's Barmy Army' could muster.

A couple of hours before we left for the fight, I was having an overpriced beer with some of the lads when Shane walked over to the table and announced, "It looks like your mate is here, Ben." I hastily made my way to the lobby and saw William standing at the reception desk, holding a white envelope that evidently contained tickets for the show. "Alright William...? Long time no see...?"

"Oh, Hi Ben... Listen, I just need to sell these and then we can meet up later and I'll sort you out."

He spoke as if he was in a desperate hurry and made no allusion to his 'radio silence' for the last several weeks. It wasn't what I wanted to hear but at least he was staying in the same hotel which was a vast improvement on the situation as it previously stood. Lest I should fall prey to an attack of hypocrisy, I am forced to acknowledge that William's behaviour wasn't hugely dissimilar to mine. We were both ducking and diving, trying to stay one step ahead of the game and hoping to emerge smelling of roses. Retrospectively, the phrase 'hoist by your own petard' springs to mind.

Our tickets turned out to be standing room only but nobody complained and a great night was had by all. Murray, for his part, put up a fantastically gusty effort before capitulating in the 11th round, the longest that Golovkin had yet been extended in defence of his various middleweight crowns. As the French referee moved in to rescue a challenger who was bloody but unbowed, I had occasion to recall one of the old man's favourite phrases to describe such spirited resistance in the face of the inevitable: 'He gave it his all and it never looked like being enough.' I was still drinking in the hotel bar at 3am with Daily Mail journalist, Jeff Powell, and a few stragglers when Martin walked in wearing dark shades to hide his copious facial bruises. Collectively, we stood to attention and gave him the ovation that he richly deserved.

The next morning, I reported for breakfast and immediately became aware of a conflagration involving William, a portly Scottish gentleman, 2 police officers and 3 aggressive looking Germans with cropped haircuts. He had the bleary eyed look of a man who had been drinking all night and, upon catching sight of me, immediately appealed for moral support.

"Ben…! Can you believe this..? These Neo-Nazis are threatening us and the police don't even care..!"

I admitted that it all sounded terribly absorbing but was more interested in the small matter of my outstanding readies at this point. Ignoring my polite enquiry, he continued to bang about the Nazis and the flagrant inadequacies of Monaco law enforcement. It was true that the officers didn't seem overly sympathetic to his plight. His appearance and general manner just didn't engender compassion in most people. In due course, the argument petered out as the police left and William careened into the elevator, presumably in search of his bed. We were due to leave shortly in order to catch a train to Nice and there was still no resolution regarding the debt. After breakfast, having ascertained that he was resident in Room 915, George Hillyard and I went to pay our bearded friend a visit in a last gasp attempt to extract some restitution. I knocked on the door and heard him groan softly as if subject to unreasonable harassment from cruel racketeers. Eventually, he appeared in his boxer shorts and mumbled something about an immediate bank transfer as soon as he was back on English soil. Something in our body language must have suggested a degree of menace as he suddenly picked up a pair of jeans off the bed and began rummaging in the pockets. Plucking out the princely sum of 30 Euros, he claimed, "That's all I've got right now."

I accepted the pittance and walked away without further ado with George in hot pursuit. Back on the ground floor, everyone was packed and ready to go, when I asked, "Does anyone fancy a quick beer for the road..?" Upon receiving an enthusiastic show of hands, I ordered 11 pints of lager and signed the bill in the name of William, Room 915. All things considered, it was the least I could do.

21/ COME DINE WITH ME

Not content with injecting my peculiar brand of chaos into the big fight package tour concept, I saw no reason why the legends after dinner circuit couldn't benefit from my involvement and vice versa. When Nigel Benn's UK agent approached me about bringing the 'Dark Destroyer' back to his old stomping ground of Essex, he insisted that it was a 'golden opportunity.' Taking him at his word, I can only assume in hindsight that I was the proud owner of an inverse Midas touch.

In case you're curious, after getting back from Monte Carlo, I spent the next several weeks staying in various cheap international backpacker hostels in Central London. I was still homeless when my welterweight prospect, Robert Asagba, made a winning pro debut at the York Hall on March 7, 2015. It was a ludicrous situation to be in, posing for victory pictures in ring centre and celebrating in the local pubs before booking myself a bed wherever there might be cheap availability at closing time. I wasn't street homeless or entirely without income and most of my things were safely in storage but the pressure of treading water and maintaining the facade of normality was arguably more stressful than the lot of a regular down and out. Though it all, I was incapable of admitting that I had lost control of my life and needed help

When the grand dinner with Nigel Benn came around in October, I was staying with a friend in the rural backwater of Chorleywood. John was a good man who put me up for several months and asked for nothing in return bar the occasional training session in the interests of getting closer to the aesthetic of his lightweight days at Westminster ABC. He was a successful businessman, single father and boxing fanatic who only tired of my company when our mutual midweek drinking became a tad excessive. After several nights of indulgence in a row, he would gently suggest that we ought to 'cut out the sessions indoors' but he might as well have asked me to stop breathing.

I got the impression that Nigel didn't much care for me when we met at the Prince Regent Hotel in Chigwell a few days before the event. The tour had been organised by a guy called Mark, a master of ceremonies, comedian and memorabilia dealer whom I had met through Chrissy Morton, the queen of white collar boxing in East London. Nigel was used to being interviewed by Mark for such appearances and didn't seem overly keen on a deviation from that format. When informed that I would be asking the questions on the night he eyed me sceptically and enquired, "But do you know the ins and outs..?"

"Of your career...? Yes." I replied.

"Yeah, but it's not just about my career. What about my suicide attempt.. ? My conversion...? If it's just boxing then it will be 'same old, same old'.."

I had in fact read his autobiography that detailed the darker times, culminating in a bid to end it all on Streatham Common with a combination of sleeping pills and carbon monoxide poisoning. Suspecting that he and Mark had crafted a well rehearsed cabaret of tear jerking cliches and motivational sound bytes, I was mildly affronted at the suggestion that I wasn't up to the job. It occurred to me that there might be another problem in the shape of a former associate on the guest list. They had been inseparable in the first phase of the glory days before falling out shortly after his fight with Robbie Sims. How did he feel about the man he had once regarded as a surrogate older brother, 25 years on...?

"I can't stand him." (He elaborated on the reason for his antipathy but since the allegation is almost certainly libellous, it shall not appear here.)

"So, I'm guessing you're not cool with him attending on Thursday night...?"

"Nah, you invite who you like, mate. I've got Jesus and don't need no one else," he asserted. I didn't know it at the time but this was pure recovery thinking, which espoused the banishing of resentments for the sake of one's peace of mind. His tetchiness towards me aside, I could sense that here was a happy man who had negotiated his own private hell and come out the other side.

I arrived at the venue on Thursday October 15 at 6pm with £700 in my pocket and 10 bottles of cheap champagne, purchased from the local branch of Lidl not an hour before. I still owed the Prince Regent £1500 for the catering and they were refusing to serve so much as a bowl of French onion soup until it was paid in full. Nigel's fee for the night was £5000, every penny of which remained outstanding 90 minutes before his arrival. Under normal circumstances, it would already have been paid but being as Mark and I were reasonably well acquainted, we had proceeded on the basis of a handshake. Essentially, I needed to raise almost 6 thousand pounds in the next 4 hours in order to avoid a public humiliation. That revenue would need to come from sales on the door, raffle tickets, photography and the all important kick back from the auction. I paced around the empty function suite with 30 tables set expectantly beneath the chandeliers and said a silent prayer to the Gods of fiscal fortitude.

As the place filled up with guests, the glamour girls did a fantastic job of selling raffle tickets and I felt marginally better when the lovely Danni handed me a fat white envelope containing enough cash to square up the bill for the food and waitress service. I was by no means out of the woods but at least we had ensured that nobody would be going hungry. Oblivious to my concerns, Alan Minter, Colin McMillan, Herol Graham and Jimmy Tibbs mingled with fans in the V.I.P reception area sipping champagne – or lemonade in Alan's case due to an extended struggle with the booze that had kept him out of the public eye for many years. Also present was Rod Douglas who had beaten Nigel twice as an amateur before his paid career was cruelly curtailed when he suffered a bleed on the brain during an abortive challenge for Herol's British title in 1989. A quarter of a century down the line, neither man was in a great place financially or emotionally, it seemed. Jealously would be the wrong word but the palpable sense of injustice – that they would never command 5 thousand pounds for a few hours of their time – was impossible to ignore.

The highlight of the night was a planned surprise appearance from Michael Watson during dinner. Essentially robbed of his youth and athleticism in a near tragic rematch with Chris Eubank at White Hart Lane in 1991, it was hard to say if Michael had been more or less fortunate than Rod or Herol. Physically, he was less abled but his inspirational struggle in the face of adversity had made him a hero and a roaring ovation ensued as he walked doggedly down the aisle supported by carer, Lenny Ballack, with the Rocky theme playing over the tannoy. Upon catching sight of his former conqueror, the Dark Destroyer jumped off the dais and provided a sturdy escort onto the stage. Once there, the two warriors embraced in one of those beautiful snapshot moments that makes us so misty eyed about a corrupt and ruthless business that so often takes vastly more than it gives.

My share of the photo profits came to just under £900. I still hadn't found the courage to count the door receipts but the ample bulge in my suit trouser pocket made me feel as if we were close to the target. A decent auction would see my home and dry, I reckoned. Aware of my predicament, Mick bought a Muhammad Ali bust that he probably didn't urgently need for a thousand pounds cash. A pair of authentic Nigel Benn shorts and a signed Oscar De La Hoya pic were also snapped up but – as if we didn't have enough problems – a malfunction of the PDQ machine prevented them from being paid for on the night. The grand finale of the interview was scheduled after a 15 minute recess and I was obliged to give Nigel his dough before he came back on stage. To that end, Mark and I retired to a dark cupboard sized room in order to total up the receipts in private. At this point, he was positively wracked with stress and anxiety, openly cursing the poor judgement that had allowed him to trust me in the first place. On two occasions, he lost count of the pig choking ream of notes and lamented, "I'm getting chest pans over this…!" Finally, it was ascertained that we had 4 thousand and 20 pounds. I was pleasantly surprised that we hadn't fallen shorter but Mark had built a good reputation in the industry over the years and was damned if he would see it sullied on account of my remedial financial planning.

"Ben, you are a GRAND short. What do you intend to do…?"

I asked if I had any leeway to raise the rest of the cash.

"If I tell Nigel you've only got 4K he might walk out of here without doing the interview. And he'd be perfectly within his rights."

I went for a walk to clear my head, knowing that the star of the show was upstairs in the Duchess suite with bouncers Big Larry and his equally humongous colleague, blissfully unaware of the backstage crisis. With a display of loyalty that went way beyond the call of friendship, John stepped up and put in the £1000 required to make up the contracted appearance fee. The day was saved and, once again, the most flattering portrait emerged of a 'successful' entrepreneur living out his dreams and rubbing shoulders with icons. It was an illusion consistently maintained at the expense of decent people who had worked hard for their money and surely had more noble causes to fritter it on than the bolstering of my ego. The only sensible reason for hosting such an event, with all its attendant headaches, was to make a decent profit. I had finished up with 20 quid and three bottles of cheap champagne leftover from the meet and greet. With the adulation still ringing in my ears, I made short work of the unwanted 'bubbly' with an ex pro named Joe Catchpole who conveniently lived in the area and let me crash on the sofa.

3 weeks later, I Interviewed Michael Watson at the Victoria pub in a pretty riverside town in Hertfordshire called Ware. Publican Jim was boxing mad and had offered me an agreeable fee

to host an intimate evening with a man who had effectively garnered the status of martyrdom in British boxing circles. It was Michael's misfortune that led to the mandatory presence of paramedics at all UK professional boxing shows, an advancement that almost certainly saved the life of Spencer Oliver half a dozen years later. I had been out in Camden Town the night before and steadily drinking all day to maintain an even keel. As unworthy as it may sound, any fears I had about sounding half cut when talking into the microphone were allayed by Michael's understandably slurred speech pattern. If one was feeling a little fragile then he was the perfect dance partner.

At one point, he noticed the writer Ian Probert in the audience and a poignant reunion ensued. The two had forged a close friendship in the late 1980s when Ian was a budding boxing journalist and it was Michael's near death experience in the ring that had soured him on what was – by his own admission – a 'reluctant obsession' with the sweet science. His journey of disillusionment is wonderfully described in the autobiographical 'Rope Burns', which remains one of the finest boxing books I have ever read. Latterly, he would credit me with giving him the confidence to pen a sequel called 'Dangerous' in which this very scene is described from his perspective.

With the interview being hugely well received, I celebrated into the small hours with an amalgamation of beer and spirits plus a rendition of my karaoke staple, 'A Town Called Malice.' With no danger of getting back to London, I slept at the house of a friend who lived locally but struggle to recall specific details beyond that bare fact. What I do know is that the Watson event took place on a Saturday night and I got back to Chorleywood on the Sunday evening but Monday through Thursday of the following week remain a blur. Because I didn't show up at the gym or post on social media for 96 hours, rumours abounded concerning my disappearance or possible demise. I came to on the Friday morning, sick as a dog in John's spare room and suddenly remembered that I had agreed to interview Anthony Joshua at the old West Ham Boleyn ground that very night.

At some point during a several day bender, an alcoholic will experience a reaction that is far beyond the realm of a hangover. I was caked in a cold sweat and could hear imaginary music droning relentlessly inside my skull like a tormenting children's nursery rhyme. Standing upright felt like a horrible purgatory somewhere between life and death and I honestly didn't know if I could go through with the prestigious assignment in a few hours time. I dragged myself out of bed and down to the local Co-op to purchase a couple of bottles of cider in the hope they might restore some semblance of humanity. Knocking them back steadily, I texted my friend Mark and requested an urgent meeting as soon as he finished work.

Mark worked as a trader for a big firm near Cannon Street Station and was well versed in the pitfalls of my alcoholism having bailed me out of numerous scrapes over the years. To this day, he remains one of the best and most loyal people in my life. Standing before him on Dowgate Hill like a one man identity parade, I asked if I looked in a fit state to interview the future Heavyweight Champion of the World before a live audience. He scanned me up and down before concluding, "I think you can do it."

Figuring that such an important role must have entitled me to a plus one, I asked him to come along for moral support. I still felt decidedly ropey and insisted we stop at a pub on Bishopsgate so I could neck another pint before continuing to Upton Park. The event's promoter, Lee Eaton, expressed his relief that I had kept the appointment and claimed to have heard 'all sorts' on the grapevine since I had gone incommunicado. Suddenly, I got a video call from Big Larry who had a fight the next day in Bristol and wanted to know if I would still be working his corner. I had forgotten all about that. Starting to feel my legs underneath me, I had 2 pints of Guinness and managed to eat some of the pie and mash that was served in keeping with the Cockney football ambience. In was the first proper meal I had eaten in days.

By the time I was seated on the stage with the incumbent Golden Boy of British boxing, a remarkable transformation had occurred. The weight of the cordless microphone and its amplification of my voice seemed to serve as an anchor to reality and I began to speak with confidence and aplomb. Going for the jugular, I suggested that the star guest had been more than a tad fortunate to progress beyond the first series of the 2012 Olympics after a disputed win over the Cuban, Erislandy Savon. Demure and casual in charcoal grey trousers and a fitted black shirt, he smiled and conceded, "I hear what you're sayin' but he can't come to my town and expect any favours." AJ was an out and out charmer and often used the politician's trick of throwing a question back at the interviewer. Warming to the task, having dealt with the more biographical aspects, I asked him about the pitfalls of fame. The media scrutiny, nocturnal temptations and fast women. "Let's face it," I continued, "You are a ludicrously good looking guy…and I can say that you because I'm secure in my sexuality..!"

The audience laughed and so did the champ as he pointed to a light skinned, pony tailed black guy in his entourage and explained, "I usually give the groupies to him." In 4 weeks time he would face Dillian Whyte in a highly anticipated grudge match for the British and Commonwealth heavyweight titles at the O2 Arena and this would be the last occasion on which he ever made an appearance for a relatively modest fee. I closed with, "LADIES AND GENTLEMEN, FUTURE HEAVYWEIGHT CHAMPION OF WORLD… ANTHONY JOSHUA…" to rapturous applause.

At no point did he appear to realise how twisted I was and I will always love him for that.

22/ DEUTSCHLAND UBER ALLES

The next day at noon, Phillip picked me up in a 7 seater MVP, also containing Big Larry, as we plotted a course to Bristol. Being so thoroughly sickened by the most recent episode, I swore in vain that I would never touch another drop of booze as long as I lived. Such promises are always pointless from the lips of an alcoholic and had I known what the day had in store for me, I'd have taken a 4 pack of Kronenbourg for emergency medicinal purposes. I felt ok when we set off but somewhere between Reading and Swindon, I began to experience what I can only assume were withdrawal symptoms from the sudden cessation of alcohol to my system. I convulsed in the passenger seat and the sweat poured in reams as I demanded that Phillip stop at the nearest service station so I could buy some water.

We pulled up at Membury Services and, remembering the comfort they had provided in days of yore, I invested in a box of Nurofen Plus. Swallowing two of the white capsule sized tablets with a bottle Volvic, I paced around the car park as Phillip and Larry exchanged quizzical glances with one another in the van. Sensing their mutual impatience, I clambered back into the vehicle and gave my consent for the driver to proceed. When the Nurofen kicked in, it only served to make me tight chested and by the time we arrived at the City Academy Sports Centre, I was pale as a ghost and struggling to breathe. I tried to put on a brave face but suddenly felt as if I was going to die and everything seemed to happen with surreal alacrity after that. I can remember nearly fainting in the main hall and a lady paramedic coming to my aid and administering a nebuliser in what amounted to a makeshift treatment room at the back of the venue. "We've never lost a patient on a Saturday night," claimed her male colleague in an effort to inject humour into the situation.

While Larry went through the process of losing yet another 4 round decision – on this occasion to one Cassius Chaney – I was flat on my back in the ambulance intended for worst cases scenarios in combat. Working as chief second in my stead was

Dominic Ingle , son of the legendary Brendan, and he seemed to form a low opinion of me, based chiefly on this debacle. The illness was breathing down my neck and word was getting out in the circles that I had a problem. Needless to say, I didn't get my 10 percent and the journey back to Chorleywood was rather strained. In any case, Larry only fought one more time, although to call if fighting would be unforgivably hyperbolic. If his 106 second capitulation to Hughie Fury live on Channel 5, three weeks later, wasn't the worst televised performance in boxing history then I have certainly yet to see its inferior.

On the plus side. I managed to abstain for another 11 days, until Shaun and I flew to Stuttgart. Of all the comically disastrous episodes that unfolded during my years in the madness, the Fury – Klitschko weekend arguably stands alone. The fight had originally been scheduled for October 24 and, with that date in mind, I put a package deal together at £600 per head. When Klitschko allegedly injured his calf whilst disembarking from an aircraft, causing the fight's postponement, everybody who had booked on the original trip pulled out – with the exception of Shaun from Burton upon Trent. I had lost money on non refundable flights and hotel bookings and was strongly inclined to abandon the project until Shaun stressed that it was his lifelong dream to attend a world heavyweight championship fight. Feeling obliged to honour the agreement and deliver his fantasy, I resolved to find the cheapest possible contingency.

Shaun – a slightly built, affable West Midlander with a hairline that had largely given up the ghost – arrived in London on Wednesday November 25 in order to do a bit of sight seeing ahead of the trip. When he asked which airport we would be flying from, I skirted around the issue and attempted to change the subject as I had yet to procure our flights for the following day. To that end, I spent several hours on Skyscanner that night, exploring every possible route within the parameters of my meagre budget, even considering a flight to Nice with a connecting train at one point.

Flights to Düsseldorf were prohibitively expensive so close to the big fight but I found a good deal on 2 returns to Stuttgart, which was only 250 miles away when all said and done. As ridiculous as it sounds, I was genuinely planning for us to bunk the train to Düsseldorf, since I had often found European transport networks to be rather lazily administrated. Looking back, it wasn't the kind of behaviour one would expect from a reputable tour operator.

The next day, I took Shaun for a spot of lunch in Nico's Caff near Bethnal Green Tube station and offered to give him an impromptu tour of the East End before we made our way to Stanstead. Sensing his need for some degree of assurance, I showed him the flight confirmation email on my phone. Studying the text on the screen, his eyes suddenly narrowed in an expression of mild concern:

"But this says GATWICK."

A cursory inspection proved him right. What can one say when the customer points out such a blatant oversight….? Groping for a positive spin on such naked incompetence, I replied:

"Well, Thank God I had the presence of mind to show it to you. In that case, we'd better go to Gatwick…!"

At this point, he simply had to be questioning the wisdom of doing business with a man who booked 11th hour flights to the wrong city and didn't even know which airport we were departing from. In an effort to win back his confidence, I turned on the charm, waxing lyrical about the intertwined history of East London boxing and villainy as we strolled down the Bethnal Green Road, past the Repton and up Vallance road to the Blind Beggar. He ordered a pint of lager and asked, "What are you having, Ben..?"

I ought to have to told him that I had a chronic drink problem and had currently managed 12 days off the sauce but it seemed like a heavy conversation to get into with a relative stranger. Not desiring to be a killjoy, I relented, "I'll have a pint of Kronenbourg, please, Shaun…"

As soon as I took the first sip, our mutual fates were sealed. The next 3 days would be an out and out car crash and nothing that could conceivably go wrong would fail to do so. More pints were downed before a hasty conveyance to Gatwick via from London Bridge as the first major drama of the trip presented itself. Believing we had ample time for another pint before boarding, we arrived at the gate to find it had closed and the crew were refusing to accept any more passengers. Remonstrations followed and the captain relented until another problem became apparent. For reasons unknown, my passport picture had become unrecognisably blurred since I had last flown at the start of the year. It appeared as if some kind of liquid had infiltrated the thin layer of plastic, leaving my identifying image as featureless as an abstract Picasso. "I'm afraid you can't possibly travel with this, sir," said the lady border control officer before turning to Shaun and asking, "Are you prepared to travel without this gentleman, sir..?"

Looking like a kid about to be abandoned by his mother on the first day at big school, Shaun shook his head vociferously. I got the impression that he had seldom been abroad and would have no idea how to fend for himself in a foreign country. Against the odds, after further arbitration, it was agreed that I would be allowed to fly on the understanding that I got a new passport as soon as possible. As we sprinted down the gangway, Shaun's relief manifested itself in a playful threat. "Ben, I'm going to fucking kill you in a minute. You came highly recommended…!"

Once in the air, I decided it was time to switch to the whisky and cokes since 330 ml cans of Heineken were clearly the preserve of the grossly effeminate drinker. We touched down in Stuttgart a 100 minutes later in the kind of condition that might have seen us barred from any nightclub with reasonable standards of admission. After going through the same rigmarole of explanation as regards my passport, I told Shaun that we would need to find a source of Wi-Fi in the airport in order for me to book a hotel for the night. 3 hours earlier, he might have been aghast at the slapdash logistics but, by now, he was too drunk to care. I managed to get online via the Hertz Car Rental concession but could only seem to maintain the connection by crouching low on my haunches which made the situation look even more ridiculous than it already was.

I booked a double room at a modestly priced hotel in the city centre and we took a taxi downtown. When we arrived, the receptionist was sorry to report that I had actually booked for the following week and there were no vacancies on this particular evening. Asking if I could connect to the Wi-Fi for a moment, I found an alternative located right next to the airport we had just come from. In the interests of economy, I suggested we go by train this time after visiting the German equivalent of an off license to pick up some more beers. The airport hotel was a Travelodge type affair and we were both enamoured to find an apparently free bottle of red wine in the sterile tidy room. It was becoming apparent that Shaun and I had one thing in common, at least, in the shape of an unquenchable thirst for ethyl alcohol in its various retail forms. We had bonded by now and he seemed to be having a whale of a time as we ploughed through the wine and beer before nodding off in adjacent beds.

The next morning, we had breakfast in the downstairs restaurant before heading back into town for a hair of the dog. As soon as we were sitting comfortably in a downmarket watering hole near Stuttgart Central Station, I explained the necessary plan of campaign to my new sidekick in hushed tones. We would board the next train bound for Düsseldorf without purchasing tickets in advance and hope to avoid unwanted attention. It went without saying that we would also require several cans of lager – no less than 5 percent by volume – as a means of ensuring that the 3 hour journey didn't drag too laboriously. Within 20 minutes of our departure, we were accosted by 2 officious looking train guards who predictably demanded payment – or evidence thereof – if we desired to reach the intended terminus. Since I had already run out of liquid cash, poor Shaun was obliged to shell out for two single fares at the equivalent of £60 each. Although I didn't have money, I was in possession of 5 tickets for the fight and it was my intention to sell 3 of them at the other end in order to compensate Shaun for these extraneous expenses. Despite his lack of experience in context, he must have been aware that this was not how an 'all inclusive' package was supposed to work.

Upon reaching Düsseldorf, a motel was found in the city centre, again at Shaun's expense whilst I waited on my projected windfall. The continued damage to his exchequer notwithstanding, he emerged from the shower in good spirits and asked if I could furnish him with one of the fight tickets so that he might share the image on Facebook. It was a harmless request and one that I would have been only too delighted to accede to under different circumstances. Placing my hand in the inside pocket of my blazer, I encountered a worrying vacuum where the white envelope containing our tickets ought to have been. Discovering that they weren't in my trouser pockets either, I turned my bag out onto the carpet and began to search through its contents as casually as I could while Shaun looked on with muted trepidation. If the scene had been mocked up for a classic English farce, one might have thought it over the top but, unfortunately, this was happening for real. Finally, I broke the silence:

"Shaun.. There's no easy way to this…. I think I've left the tickets on the fucking train…!"

The colour drained from his face but he said nothing. Faithful to my 'never say die attitude', I still thought there might be a resolution. I had email receipts for the tickets I had purchased on Viagogo along with the block and seat numbers. The best thing we could do, I surmised, was to report to the Espirit Arena in the morning and see if they could replace the tickets. Surely it was no big deal in an increasingly virtual world…? Having come all this way via an expensively circuitous route – quite possibly for sod all – Shaun didn't seem overly optimistic. Based on everything he had seen in the last 48 hours, I could hardly blame him.

We endured a difficult couple of hours during which neither one of us said a great deal before he went downstairs and returned with a bottle of white wine from the bar. It was polished off in short order and the ritual was repeated until, midway through the fourth bottle, neither one of us much cared about the lost tickets or the death of a dream. We laughed and joked like a pair of street drunks, temporarily oblivious to our unenviable plight and in strong agreement that most people took life far too seriously.

The only downside to drowning one's sorrows is that they invariably find a life jacket in the morning. It was a bleak day outside and it suddenly occurred to me that I was stranded and potless in an unfamiliar German city with an unwitting companion who had every excuse to take me to the small claims court. I wondered for a moment if my luck had finally run out before quickly getting a hold of myself and banishing the negative thoughts. These were the championship rounds and it was time to bite down on the gum-shield. I hit the shower and googled directions to the venue which turned out to be a 30 minute train ride away. Unlike the traditional English jobsworth, the pleasantly overweight fellow in the box office seemed genuinely empathetic to our misfortune and explored every possible avenue through which our paper tickets might be replaced. He was literally prepared to go the extra mile, at one point walking us from one end of the complex to the other in order to speak to a person of higher authority. Unfortunately, because I had used a third party site, there was nothing they could do besides offer us some new tickets at face value. Shaun hadn't come 500 miles just to get slaughtered on overpriced Liebfraumilch and duly forked out another £200 to ensure our presence in the Arena when the first bell rang. Things hadn't gone entirely to plan but we would sort this mess out back in Blighty, I promised.

With several hours to kill, we ventured to the Aldstadt district and met up with a Facebook friend of mine called Alex Voce who was also going to the fight. Initially, Alex and I had been at loggerheads on account of his passionate animus toward Muhammad Ali but a mutual respect was forged thereafter. We must have enjoyed several rounds and the next thing I knew, night had fallen over the vibrant narrow streets and Alex was nowhere to be seen. Concluding that it was high time we repaired to the stadium, I urged Shaun to finish his beer and prepare for the joys of the Stadtbahn . I can remember arriving at the plush 50, 000 seater arena and drinking another pint during one of the undercard fights – probably Jono Carrol vs a Honduran fighter with 4 names if boxrec can be trusted. Aside from that, I have no sharp recollections bar the velvet tones of Michael Buffer cutting through the fog of inebriation to confirm, "ALL THREE SCORES TO THE WINNER BY UNANIMOUS DECISION… FROM THE UNITED KINGDOM…."

The remainder of the announcement was lost as the British fans went berserk and Shaun and I embraced as if something far more advantageous to our lives had just occurred. With probably less than perfect diction, I was keen to stress that he had hereby witnessed a moment in sporting history and one couldn't put a price on that. Certainly, my initial estimate of £600 had proven to be woefully conservative. In an effort to avoid yet more expenses, I suggested we get an overnight train back to Stuttgart rather than book another night at the Inn. I figured we had a better chance of evading the fare during the graveyard shift and was hoping to spare Shaun's credit card from further abuse.

We picked up our bags from the motel luggage room and walked to the station, stopping at a liquor store en route where

I attempted to buy a bottle of Jim Beam and was pleasantly surprised to see the card transaction go through. There were no trains going anywhere until 3am and as we waited on the concourse, passing the Bourbon back and forth, I saw several acquaintances from the UK boxing fraternity heading to the airport. On the proviso that any movement represented progress, we jumped on the first outbound service without checking where it was going, the Jim Beam no doubt impairing my ability to make prudent decisions. At 5am, we woke up in what turned out to be Cologne with a trio of inspectors in grey uniforms standing over us on a stationary train. Karma was clearly punishing us for reasons best known to itself.

Although 2 hours had plainly elapsed, we were only 50 miles closer to Stuttgart and to make matters worse, the 3 stooges expected us to pay for such minuscule progress. Shaun handed over his bank card but he was a broken man by now, quite devoid of zest and humanity. He shivered copiously and continually muttered, "I just wanna' go 'ome.." in a manner that stuck me as genuinely poignant. By now, I wanted much the same thing but it would be another hour before the next train and I had run out of comforting things to say.

I was still drinking the dregs of Jim Beam as we stood in line at Stuttgart Airport, waiting to clear security. Once again the irrevocably distorted passport photograph was queried at the gate but, ultimately, I was England's problem and Germany knew it. Just to put the tin lid on the package tour from hell, the flight back to Heathrow was marred by the worst turbulence I have ever experienced. I wasn't even sure if Shaun had ever been on an aeroplane until a few days ago and he didn't appear to be handling it well. By the time we landed and said our goodbyes on a grey Sunday afternoon, he looked positively shell shocked and I was quite certain that I would never hear from him again.

I was proven wrong a week later when I received a message on Facebook that read as follows:

'Ben, you discussed with me some form of refund. Please don't be offended but I won't accept any such thing. Germany was awesome… The only thing I ask is that you keep me in the loop. It was all worth it to me.'

By way of a postscript, it might interest you to know that Shaun went to AA a year later and got sober. We are still in touch today and I am delighted that he has found recovery and all its attendant gifts. Although we often reminisce about our chaotic German odyssey, I am confident that neither one of us would care to revisit those days.

23/ TICKET GATE

Waking up in Hainault Station at 6 am on Christmas morning is bad enough but the sudden realisation that one is imprisoned within its confines is arguably even more deflating. Underdressed and bitterly cold, I pressed the green emergency button on the white circular 'Help Point' and hoped for a response:

"Hello.. Control room.." (Female voice.)

"Hello… I'm afraid to say that I'm stuck inside Hainault Station. The shutters are down and I can't get out."

"How did you get in..?"

"To be honest with you, I'm not sure. I had a few drinks last night."

"Ok, if you go down to the exit, I'll send someone to let you out. It might take a little while today."

An hour later, a biracial duo of police officers arrived and asked a few typically awkward questions, before slicing off the padlock with bolt cutters to facilitate my exit. The most awkward question related to my address. Reluctant to admit that I had nowhere to go, I gave Diana's postcode and was allowed to get on my way after a crackling exchange on the white cop's radio confirmed that I was not a wanted man. Before Old Bill arrived, I had taken the precaution of cashing in my Oyster Card for the £5 refund so I would have enough for a few cans of strong cider upon my release. To cut a long story short, I had worn out my welcome in Chorleywood and had no money for cheap accommodation. All I could remember of Christmas Eve was endlessly ricocheting between Ealing Broadway and Epping on the Central Line whilst drinking red wine before evidently coming to a halt at Hainault some time after midnight.

Since there was no public transport on Christmas day, I walked 4 miles to Wanstead and saw that the George pub opposite the station was open for business. Thinking that I might see someone I knew who would buy me a drink, I ventured inside and discreetly picked up an empty pint glass from one of the tables. I took the glass to the toilets and rinsed it clean before pouring one of my cans of Strongbow Super into it and returning to the bar as if I were a regular patron having a quick Christmas drink. Unfortunately, the only people boozing at J.D Wetherspoons' pleasure before 10am on a Yuletide morn were old age pensioners and fellow loners and I didn't have a previous acquaintance with any of them. Admitting defeat, I finished my bogus looking pint and walked another 4 miles to Stratford.

I had no particular reason to go to Stratford besides the familiarity it represented and – after 6 cans of rocket fuel – my sense of air and grace was sufficiently depleted for me to lie down with the homeless people in the mall. Perhaps I should say the other homeless people. Certainly the young black girl who was evidently part of a charitable enterprise handing out Christmas dinners to the needy made no distinction as she offered me an approximation of a Sunday roast on a paper plate covered with cellophane. I was tired and hungry and saw no advantage in refusing to wear a cap that fitted so snugly at that precise moment in time. I ate the food in its entirety and fell asleep for a few hours, longing for oblivion.

It was dark when I awoke and found myself instinctively heading in the direction of Maitland Road, convinced that binary parenthood must count for something. Upon arrival, I pressed the buzzer and heard evidence of a festive gathering in the ground floor flat that I had briefly called home. When Diana appeared in the doorway, I kept it short and sweet.

"Please help me…"

"Ok," she agreed, "But behave yourself. You can sleep in Joseph's room."

I crawled under the covers with my elder, autistic son as the sounds of music, laughter and socialising filtered through the wall. The noise of other people's innocent merriment seemed to serve as a goading reminder that I had fucked everything up and surrendered my entitlement to any kind of life. The formerly generous reserves of optimism and self belief were now exhausted and I just didn't care if I woke up in the morning or not.

When I did wake up in the morning, Diana lent me some money and I went to stay with my friend Tony Roberts in Sutton for a few days. Tony, a huge boxing fan and something of a local legend, gave me thirty quid and told me to get myself a new outfit from Primark, adding, "I don't ever want to hear about it again." In recovery circles, it is said that an alcoholic must hit rock bottom before he or she is ready to get sober. In truth, I think most of us have several rock bottoms before the miracle occurs. This ought to have been the turning point for me but after the traditional 3 day period of recuperation, I continued to drink. Perhaps seeking appropriate camouflage for my behaviours, I found a house share in Plaistow with a bunch of 20 something stoners who were too absorbed in their own cycle of spliffs, gaming and take away deliveries to pay any mind to my nightly excesses. Potentially, it was a lovely house but under their lackadaisical stewardship, it resembled the set of 'The Young Ones.' The fact that I felt comfortable in such an environment is damning enough in itself.

By 2016, I was firmly entrenched in the business of ticket brokering for big fights on both sides of the Atlantic. I had the connections and a reputation in the industry that remained spotless despite the mess of my personal life. When Anthony Joshua fought Charles Martin for the IBF title in April, I was put in touch with a member of his inner circle known as 'King.' The deal was simple enough. King would sell me the tickets at £20 more than the face value and I would add my own commission when I sold them on to the punters. There was a huge demand for the fight – in spite of Martin's dubious credentials – and once again I was in possession of relatively large amounts of cash that didn't belong to me. The Vegas and Monte Carlo trips had plunged me into debt – as had the Nigel Benn night – and it's fair to say that Düsseldorf had hardly been a money spinner. With my 'robbing Peter to pay Paul' ethos, it was only a matter of time before the situation spiralled out of control.

Joshua destroyed Martin in 2 rounds at a packed out O2 Arena on a night that I remember better than the German escapade but only marginally so. When the time came to settle up, I strategically stalled King with whatever plausible nonsense I could think of whilst waiting for some investment to come through for a Frank Bruno night in several weeks time. I borrowed heavily to stage an event that was only a cosmetic success and used some of the money to pay King before he became too suspicious or disgruntled. When AJ made his first defence two months later vs Dominic Breazeale, we did the same deal although, on this occasion, I was banned from attending the show.

4 days before the fight, on Tuesday June 21, Matchroom staged a public workout at York Hall that also featured a pair of 6 rounders involving Craig Richards and Ohara Davies. I had been drinking all afternoon in nearby Hoxton with Kat and a South African who had recently attached himself to my every endeavour and our attendance at the free event was inadvisable at best. When Kat went home at around 5pm, the South African and I grabbed some cans of lager before repairing to Bethnal Green on foot, decidedly worse for wear. When we arrived, my friend Cherie was waiting for us outside the venue, which probably increased the potential for some kind of ruckus. Nicknamed the 'Pitbull', she was a street kid from Thamesmead with a heart of gold and had come to see me as a surrogate father since we'd met at the Lansbury Gym, the previous year. Aware of the pedestal that I occupied in her perception, it was perhaps inevitable that I would seek to show off.

My first issue was the lack of backstage access afforded to us upon entry. I argued with a young security guard and implied that he was clearly no boxing fan if he didn't recognise me, which was especially absurd even allowing for my intoxication. Fortunately – or perhaps unfortunately – Spencer alleviated the situation by procuring V.I.P passes for me and the Pitbull which I immediately waved at the security lad in a gesture of mocking triumph. As we descended the staircase leading to the traditional 'away' dressing room, Dilian Whyte was being interviewed by Kugan Cassius ahead of his own appearance on the big show. Positioning myself as next in line for an audience with the heavyweight contender, I plugged my phone charger into a nearby socket just as AJ and his entourage arrived. Knowing of my aversion to the 'alphabet soup' situation in world boxing, King handed me the IBF belt for an ironic photo opportunity whilst a young man, about 22 years old, suddenly insisted that everybody clear the area. I'd never laid eyes on Frank Smith before and had no idea of his burgeoning importance within the Matchroom Boxing organisation. Consequently, I treated him with the kind of disdain one might reserve for a school prefect and declared that I would linger wherever I damn well pleased until such time as he had started shaving. A stand off ensued as several of the larger members of the SAUK security team sought to enforce their fresh faced paymaster's wishes whilst I continued to stand my ground. Eventually, I agreed to remove myself from the vicinity but not before making several new enemies and establishing myself as a thoroughly marked man. Looking back, it's a wonder that I wasn't ejected there and then

When the show concluded at around 10pm, I attempted to get a backstage interview with Eddie Hearn only to find my access barred by Frank Smith and a massive security guard who went by the name of Brown James. There was a scuffle as somebody tried to rip the 'ACCESS ALL AREAS' laminate from my neck but I was clearly unacquainted with the concept of quitting whilst one is ahead. My sense of entitlement was so outrageously tumescent at this point that I genuinely believed the Matchroom Supremo would happily grant an interview to a drunken social media guru who had been an absolute nuisance from the very moment he entered the building and was now physically wrestling with security. When young Mr. Smith attempted to impose his authority on the situation, I simply ignored him and walked away. The Pitbull and I left unmolested but I was too drunk to appreciate the extent of the damage I had done. For good measure, I posted about the incident on Facebook, denouncing Frank Smith as 'a jobsworth who had better hope he doesn't meet me in a dark alley.'

2 days later, I rolled up at Sky Studios in Isleworth for the final presser, expecting to be let in without a hitch . As I approached the main gate, I saw Eddie Hearn who was quick to inform me, "Ben, it's not gonna' happen today, mate."

"Why not..?" I wondered.

"We'll, because of your behaviour on Tuesday night. Ben, you were paralytic and an absolute pest. I nearly come up to you at one point and told you to go home."

"I wish you had done," I admitted. "I could do without being blackballed by the major promotional powerhouse in British boxing for the next 30 odd years."

"It won't be a long term problem," he assured me. "Just keep your head down and let us get this event out of the way. I don't mind doing a piece with you out here but you can't come in, I'm afraid."

It was awfully decent of him, really. There is no way on earth that Frank Warren would have been so convivial over anything remotely similar. I was making my way off site when I bumped into Spencer who was just arriving. Upon hearing my tale of woe, he offered to get me in via the staff entrance since, being a Sky pundit, he had a bit of cachet with the front desk. Foolishly, I accepted which obviously made it appear as if I had defied Eddie's diplomatic rebuttal and was hell bent on annoying people. I was conducting an interview with Johnny Nelson after the press conference had officially terminated when a Scottish security guard in his 60s approached and said, "I'm sorry, sir, but I've been asked by Eddie Hearn to escort you off the premises." As he did so, the SAUK boys glowered at me with a communal and pugnacious contempt that finally alerted me to the gravity of the situation. I was persona non grata and had better stay away from the weigh in.

Eddie would probably have been as good as his word regarding the temporary nature of my exclusion had it not been for a far more cataclysmic shitstorm that I would soon become embroiled in. In early July, negotiations for a fight between Gennady Golovkin and Chris Eubank Jr collapsed amid the unrealistic demands of Chris Eubank Sr – at least according to Hearn. With Golovkin already committed, Eddie threw in a wild card and offered the fight to IBF Welterweight Champion, Kell Brook. Although fight fans initially thought it was fake news, the match up soon captured the British public's imagination like wildfire and it quickly became the must see event of 2016. The fight was set for September 10 at the O2 and, although he only dealt with Anthony Joshua business ordinarily, King reckoned he would be getting an allocation of tickets due to the high demand.

I was inundated with requests and began taking orders (and payments) purely on the basis of King's intimation. Essentially, I was taking money for something that was not yet in my possession but I would like to make it clear that I never intended to rip anybody off. I was caught in a vicious circle of debt that had made me constantly reliant on the next bit of business to dig me out of the hole. Much of the money that flew in for what turned out to be fictitious Brook – Golovkin tickets was used to pay back various loans and to fund an upcoming night with the legendary Michael Spinks, scheduled for September 9. I won't deny that some of it was pissed up against the wall but the majority of funds were swallowed by previous misdeeds and mistakes. I was getting in deep but still thought I could pull it off so long as King came through with the tickets. I would post them to my satisfied customers and settle up with him at a later date, using whatever stalling tactics might be required while I raised the cash. Certainly, it was never in my interests to leave everyone high and dry and screaming for blood.

By August, the stress was almost unbearable. I couldn't get hold of King and was getting the impression that he was out of the country on business. As the close aide of a celebrity world champion, he lived a jet set life style and was under no obligation to supply me with tickets for an event that he had probably underestimated in terms of market forces. Even Charlie Edwards, who was challenging for the IBF Flyweight title on the undercard was only given a hundred tickets to sell to his considerable fan base. Aside from a few peripheral punters, I had taken 3 main orders that I referred to in my notes as the Bromley Dozen, the Dunfermline 9 and the Peterborough 16. I stayed in constant touch with the representatives of each syndicate but, 3 weeks before the fight, I could tell they were getting jittery, particularly as others were confirming on social media that their tickets were in hand. By now I had given up all hope in the same regard and was merely thinking about how I might get the dough to refund everybody. Despite what would be alleged on Facebook in the coming weeks, my burden stood at £7,760. Admittedly, we weren't talking Brinks Mat type money but, since I didn't have it, it may as well have been the hundred grand of impending rumour.

I was still playing for time on the week of the fight but communications were becoming ill tempered, with Darren from Bromley threatening to go public if he wasn't rapidly reimbursed. On Monday September 5, I walked into the City Road branch of Barclays Bank to find my account had been frozen due to an allegation of fraud. Briefly, it occurred to me that the situation might work out to my advantage - by way of explaining my financial embarrassment- but I knew that it wouldn't placate anybody in the equation who mattered. On Wednesday September 7 at 6pm, as promised, Darren from Bromley posted a damning expose detailing how I had cynically conned him and 11 other pillars of the local community out of their hard earned cash. The scenario I had been dreading for 2 long years had finally come home to roost. However much of a car crash my life had been hitherto, it had never previously been exhibited on social media. If it had been then nobody would have given me the best past of 8 grand to mismanage in the first place. And in spite of my well chronicled shortcomings, I had worked hard to build a reputation in the industry that was now surely ruined beyond measure.

I woke up on Thursday September 8 at John's place in Chorleywood, in a state of utter desperation, Tables had been sold for the Michael Spinks affair the following night but there was not a chance in hell that it was going to happen. Officially, John was my co – promoter and when he received a call from Bromley Darren threatening to turn up mob handed if we went ahead with the event, he bellowed at the top of his lungs, "BRING A HUNDRED GEEZERS IF YOU LIKE... YOU WILL NOT LEAVE UNDER YOUR OWN STEAM." As much as I admired his moxie, I had no stomach for a pitched battle when I was so flagrantly in the wrong. Accordingly, I called Malcolm for the fist time in a long time and outlined my predicament as briefly as I could. Like the true friend he had always been, Malcolm transferred a thousand pounds to Bromley Darren and that was him off my back, or at least it should have been. For whatever reason, he continued to attack me online for the next several days before blocking me all together.

John drove us to a caff in Watford where he ate breakfast as I sat mute on the opposite side of the table, hiding a can of Stella and taking covert gulps whenever the waitress didn't appear to be looking in our direction. He hadn't finished his bacon and eggs when my phone rang and I stepped outside to take what I knew would be a difficult call. Former light middleweight pro, Gary Barron, was a nice fella' under normal circumstances but being fed a constant stream of bullshit for the last several weeks regarding the 16 tickets he had paid for on behalf of the Peterborough contingent had pushed him far beyond the realm of pleasantry.

"You just paid that Darren back... Where the fuck is my money...? 6 of those tickets were for Matt Skelton and he has got some 'orrible mates..! This is going to social media at 12 O' Clock. If the money ain't there then he'll be coming down and I'll be coming down with him. Don't fucking let me down..!"

I had always prided myself on being able to handle pressure but everyone has a breaking point and this was mine. Having settled up, John came outside and told me to put an official announcement on Facebook, informing people that the Spinks night was cancelled. He had already put more than 3 grand of his own money into the project and wanted nothing more to do with it. I ought to have done as he said but Facebook would be a no go zone for me in less than an hour and I just couldn't bring myself to type the words. From what I later heard, a handful of fans showed up at the Prince Regent in 36 hours time expecting an audience with the light heavyweight great but I think the 'Jinx' himself had cottoned on by that point. 2 years later, I briefly made his acquaintance in Los Angeles and found him to be extremely charmless, almost as if he knew I was the limey bastard who had stood him up in Chigwell.

John dropped me at Bushey station and handed me 40 quid from his inside blazer pocket before saying, "You'll get through this." I thanked him meekly as I got out of the car and headed straight for the nearest off license. Having stocked up on Stella, I caught a train to Stratford and proceeded to wander around East London in a daze for the next several hours with a can of lager constantly pressed to my lips. Sometime after 9pm, I rolled up at Mark's house in Buckhurst Hill, craving some words of comfort and the semblance of a solution. I hadn't come for money but he handed me £600 that he happened to have lying around, regardless. It wasn't going to touch the sides but, in such a fragile state, his loyalty almost moved me to tears.

The next 5 days were the worst of my life. Worse than the death of my father and all the gut wrenching break ups and perhaps even worse than the Great Ormond Street ordeal. Concluding that my life was over, I scarcely spoke to another living soul for more than a hundred hours, discounting shop assistants and bar tenders. On Saturday September 10 – the day of the fight – I randomly jumped on a train to Stroud although I can't recall my reasoning for doing so. Perhaps it was an attempt to reverse time and go back to a more carefree era in which hordes of people didn't want to kill me. I attempted to check in at the Imperial Hotel opposite the station but as I had no bank account and had since managed to lose my damaged passport, bureaucracy intervened and I simply caught the next train back to Paddington.

Sunday was a blur and it was only on Monday that I realised I had missed Joseph's birthday and not even sent a card. Diana had probably heard that I was in trouble and had long since relinquished any lofty expectations where I was concerned anyhow. In the parallel universe of social media, rumours abounded that I was hiding out in Spain, Monte Carlo or the Cotswolds with anything up to £100, 000 in ill gotten gains. In actual fact, I was still at the address that was being circulated online amongst the busy bodies and bandwagon jumpers who get a sexual kick from another person's downfall – especially when that person was a flash bastard like me. I kept strange hours and was instinctively wary of big black men who resembled Matt Skelton but – contrary to popular misconception – I didn't run away.

On Tuesday September 13, unable to reach me on the phone, Mark came to the house in Chesterton Road and basically ordered me to get out of bed and face the music. Aware that the journey of a thousand miles begins with a single step, he reluctantly agreed to my suggestion that we discuss the matter in the Black Lion where I could get another drink. Sick of the taste of lager, I ordered a Magners with ice and promised to turn my phone on in the morning. He warned me to brace myself for the realisation that various people whom I might have expected to remain loyal had turned against me. King of the turncoats was the South African who had seemingly hi- jacked the episode as a means of boosting his own trajectory as a moral crusader and righter of wrongs. Whatever his intentions, I think it's fair to say that even my worst enemies were able to identify him as the slime sucking filth that he undoubtedly was.

The next day, I went to the Cheapside branch of TSB and deposited £500 of the money that Mark had given me into Gary Barron's account before calling him on my mobile. I still owed him eleven hundred quid and was expecting a hostile reception but he was astonishingly calm and relaxed. So much so that I became suspicious he was playing some kind of psychological game.

"How come you're so chilled about this, Gary…?"

"Well, I know you haven't done a runner now and I appreciate the call. When can I expect the rest of it..?"

"Give me another couple of days and I'll sort it."

"Ok cheers, Ben."

With Gary apparently on side, I logged into Facebook and published a long winded apology that was far better received than I anticipated. Evidently, a lot of people were unwilling to believe that I was a straight up thief who had built a position of trust merely in order to pull off 'the long con.' In truth, there had been no con and the very idea that I would jeopardise my whole way of life for 7 and a half measly grand was comical in the extreme. I still had the Dunfermline mob to take care of but things didn't look half as bad as they had done 24 hours ago. On the downside, it was being said that I had incurred a life time ban from Matchroom Boxing shows by order of Fast Eddie himself. To this day, I don't know if Eddie actually imposed such a sanction but it seemed safe to assume that I wasn't on his Christmas card list.

24/ NIGHTMARE ON ELM PARK HIGH STREET

A month before the ticket gate scandal exploded, I had signed a contract with a fledgling media platform called Boxing Social. I received a call out of the blue one afternoon from co-founder, Neil Kettleborough, who enthusiastically pitched his plan to create the biggest digital brand in world boxing with the help of yours truly. He had been following my page for some time, he explained, and was confident that we could blow IFLtv and their nearest competitors out of the water if I came on board. After a few meetings at the parent company offices in Old Street, I signed on the dotted line despite being horribly hung over on the day in question and desperate to get to the pub for a livener. Nothing much happened in the next few weeks and then my stock plummeted so radically that my position as frontman became only marginally less tenable than Ian Huntley's prospects as a babysitter. Assuming that the contract was no longer worth the paper it had been written on, I called Neil to arrange the return of a camera they had given me for the purpose of conducting interviews.

"Not been the best of weeks for you, has it, Ben..?"

His tone was affable and had the instant effect of making me feel better.

"Look, Neil… I was just calling to apologise. I realise that we can't move forward after what's happened. I'll swing by the office and bring the camera back."

"Ben, I got you on board for a reason and I still think we can make this work. Don't worry about the camera for now. Just come in for a chat and we'll work it out."

An hour later, I was sitting in his office at 186 City Road, explaining that the figures bandied around on social media had been grossly exaggerated and I had merely run out of cash flow at an inopportune moment. Satisfied that the situation wasn't premeditated, he offered to pay off Gary Barron and deduct the money from my future earnings. That he was prepared to do that for a person he had only known for a matter of weeks - when so many had painted me worse than Hitler and the Yorkshire Ripper rolled into one - is something I've never forgotten.

Having survived the worst week of my life, it was suddenly as if the higher power sought to bathe me in the aggregate benevolence of mankind. Nestling amongst more than a hundred messages that had accumulated in my inbox during the hiatus, was a lifeline from a cab driver called Shaun. Shaun was a good friend of Jimmy Tibbs who had often frequented TKO Gym before it closed down and, essentially, he was offering to lend me as much money as I needed to get out of trouble. Mick, John and Malcolm were staunch allies but this was an almost random act of incredible kindness from a man who could not have been described as a close friend. A week later, he was as good as his word and I was able to square things with the Dunfermline 9 and most of the stragglers. Oddly, Billy Joe Saunders later told me that a notorious Glasgow gangster had contacted him regarding my whereabouts during the week of my disappearance. It sounded a little far fetched but I see no reason why Billy Joe would have made it up, despite his well known penchant for a prank,

Some said it was a comeback worthy of Lazarus but, in the real world, things continued to go downhill. The lease at Chesterton Road expired at the end of September, leading to my longest period of homelessness as I spent the next several months couch and hostel surfing. The excessive drinking continued and so did the double life. In late November, I interviewed Larry Holmes at an event in Chessington promoted by Joey Pyle Jr, son of the 1960s underworld figure of the same name. Joey had been loyal throughout my troubles and I appreciated him giving me the gig after all the negative publicity. At the conclusion of the interview on the small dimly lit stage at Hunt's Lounge, I asked the greatest heavyweight of the 1980s if there was anything else that he desired to achieve in his life..?

"I don't feel is I have to achieve anything," he admitted in that throaty, affable drawl. "Fighting has been great for me. We came from a very poor family out of Cuthbert, Georgia.. sharecroppers.....we had nothing. We had welfare, Army and Navy surplus, we wore the clothes that other people had worn and Boxing has turned that table. And I was one of the luckiest guys in the world because I met a woman that I fell in love with and she's with me right now."

As the crowd broke into spontaneous applause, I couldn't help but think he had done slightly better at life than I had up to this point. I wasn't asking for Larry Holmes' legacy or bank account but knowing where I was going to sleep that night would have been a welcome bonus. As it happened, I eschewed sleep altogether and went back to Joey's place in Mitcham where we hung out until 6am with an Irish friend of his called Anthony. In case you might be wondering, the all night session was fuelled by nothing more than whisky and exuberance since I was not into cocaine and hadn't been for years. The booze had succeeded where it's illegal cousins had ultimately failed and was finally on the verge of destroying me.

We are now entering a phase of the story involving a man who shall simply be referred to as 'The Snake.' I don't have an issue with revealing his identity in principle but would rather not sully these pages with the vowels and consonants that make up his name. The Snake was a functioning alcoholic who courted various people in the boxing industry and attempted to ingratiate himself with those in their circles. During the ticket gate scandal he had been one of my most vociferous supporters and was known to help boxers out with money when he was flush. In December, 2016 he was flat broke and had been sleeping in his car until a female friend offered to rent him a room ath er house in Dagenham. Since she was away for several weeks on holiday, he invited me to come and stay over the Christmas period, an overture that I gratefully accepted. Like me, the Snake was in a lot of debt and would constantly allude to sleepless nights, worrying about how he was going to make ends meet. I knew for a fact he was into Mick for a grand and had other creditors besides.

A couple of days before Christmas, he told me that the owner of the house had gotten wind of our arrangement and was insisting that I leave forthwith. Bizarrely, he claimed that she would be sending an envoy on Christmas Day to check that were no unsolicited guests on the premises. On Christmas morning he drank a bottle of wine before heading out to meet up with friends, advising that I must vacate the property by midday. Finding it hard to believe that any person would carry out such an errand on December 25, I resolved to make myself scarce for a few hours before returning that evening in the hope that he would allow me to stay for at least another night or two. To that end, I left my bag in the house and made a point of retaining the key when I left.

I plotted up outside Costa on Elm Park High Street, in order to access the Wi-Fi, and spent the next several hours engaging on Facebook in between constant trips to a nearby off license. I had gotten used to surviving on social media validation and booze by now and didn't view my predicament as gravely as the average person undoubtedly would have done. I returned to the house at around 6pm and found it apparently empty and in total darkness. For some reason, the key no longer worked - as if somebody had made use of a secondary lock - and so I walked back towards the High Street, cold and disconsolate.
When I got back to Costa, I noticed there was a Church on the opposite side of the street and its front door appeared to be half open. Taking advantage of a warm place to shelter, I went inside and lay down on one of benches before nodding off to sleep.

I awoke from my late siesta at 11pm and went across the road for another Facebook fix, only to find that all hell had broken loose. The Snake had accused me of stealing 2 thousand pounds from his bedroom and hordes of credulous people were denouncing me as the vilest kind of scumbag known to man. Clearly, he could no longer handle the stress of his own fiscal liabilities and had picked an easy alibi at my expense. Because he had been so supportive during the previous situation, people believed him and wondered what manner of pond life I had to be in order to be capable of such an egregious betrayal of a person who had only tried to help me. Whist I had been asleep, my phone had blown up with messages including one from The Snake himself. I invite you to reach your own conclusion as to whether it's content authentically captures the feelings of a man who has just been robbed and betrayed:

'MATE, YOU'RE DONE IN BOXING. AND IF YOU COME NEAR ME, I'LL LEAVE IT TO KEVIN AND VINNY.'

To make matters worse, even the likes of Mick and Tony Roberts were briefly taken in and I received a sardonic text from Big Larry asking, 'So what's your excuse this time..?' I was literally shaking with the most uncontrollably murderous rage I have ever experienced before or since, knowing that it was all so desperately unfair. The man who had been unable to pay back a loan of £100 to a mutual acquaintance on Christmas Eve, suddenly has 2 grand lying around his bedroom on Christmas Day until the evil vagabond disappears into the night with it..? According to the Snake's accusatory post, he was not at home at the time of writing: 'I'm out with friends right now but he'd better not be there when we get back..' it read. If he was still out with friends then it begs the question, how did he discover the 'theft' from his room in the first place…? I have accepted the vast amount of blame for all the bad things that ever happened in my life but what The Snake did that day was unconscionably evil and there is no way to sugar coat it.

I slept overnight in the church - which I obviously wouldn't have done if I'd had any money - and went back to the house on Boxing Day to return the key and pick up my bag. As he was too afraid to face me, the Snake left my bag outside and asked me to put the key through the front door. Again, it seemed like strange behaviour for a man who had allegedly been robbed only 24 hours previously by the very person standing on his doorstep. Fortunately, after the initial wave of outrage, most people in our circle came to realise that his version of events was extremely suspect and afforded me the benefit of the doubt. Things went back and forth but the preponderance of fair minded neutrals dismissed his claims in the cold light of day. With Christmas out of the way, I was able to make money again and mostly stayed at the Dictionary Hostel in Shoreditch for an average of £16 a night. Although the situation left a lot to be desired, life went on.

I was drinking in Borough Market with a friend on New Years Eve, when I got a text from The Snake, challenging me to a 'High Noon' type rendezvous as follows:

'DOUGHTY, IT'S OVER.. YOU'RE OVER..! MEET ME ONE ON ONE TOMORROW IF YOU DARE…"

The Snake was the antithesis of a fighting man and there was no way the threat would have emanated from his fingertips had he been sober. During any remotely upbeat period of my life, I would almost certainly have ignored it but I had become dangerously disenfranchised and ambivalent to the consequences of my actions. As a result, I stayed out all night, partying with strangers on the District Line before confronting my tormentor at 9am in the morning as requested. I knocked on the door of the house at Calbourne Avenue and shouted, "COME ON THEN, YOU COWARDLY CUNT…! COME DOWN HERE AND I'LL FUCKING KILL YOU..!"
In contrast to his apparent enthusiasm for a confrontation 12 hours earlier, there was no answer. I repeated the threat - or words to that effect - and suddenly noticed the flashing blue light on an otherwise unmarked police car coming down the street. I walked away slowly - betraying no urgency or guilt - unsure if I had been set up but strongly suspecting as much.

Unchallenged by plod, I got the tube to Old Street and went into the Masque Haunt for another drink. It was evident from my call log that The Snake had attempted to phone me numerous times while I was underground. He called again and when I answered, a police officer spoke, strongly recommending that I report to Dagenham Police Station to answer an allegation of making threats to kill. I took a swig of my pint and replied, "I'm in the Wetherspoons on Old Street and if you want to talk to me then I strongly recommend you come here. Failing that, I wish you luck." I hung up and didn't hear any more about it until I was arrested 12 days later at the Dictionary Hostel and taken to the Stoke Newington Cop Shop. I was detained for 9 hours but refused the standard offer of legal representation and simply told the truth when they finally got around to interviewing me. The Snake had falsely accused me of larceny, challenged me to a straightener and then gone running to the law. Even the arresting officer took a dim view of such behaviour and he was also able to confirm that no crime report was ever made regarding the fictitious theft on Christmas Day. Reluctantly, I accepted a caution for threatening words and behaviour to prevent the matter from going any further and made my way back to the Dictionary on a 243 bus. Fortunately, I was allowed to check in for another night despite the implicit dodginess of me being carted off by a trio of coppers that morning.

On the rare occasions I have seen The Snake in recent years, he has attempted to shake my hand as if nothing ever happened.

25/ THE MIRACLE

The turning point came when I met Charlie for lunch on The Cut. It was the second Thursday of March, 2017 and I had come to drop him some tickets for a show taking place at York Hall the following night. After indulging in some regular small talk, I suddenly found myself opening up about my debilitating drink problem and the thinly veiled misery it had created in my life. It so happened that Charlie had been in recovery for 3 and a half years and knew exactly what I was going through. Aware of the kid gloves approach required when coaxing an alcoholic towards that ground-breaking epiphany he asked, "Is your drinking manageable and are you enjoying it…?"

I shook my head and sighed, "No…"

"Ok," he smiled, "I'll take you to a meeting. Nothing gives me more pleasure than helping another person get sober."

He paid for lunch and told me he would be in touch. A few days later, knowing that I had no fixed abode, he arranged for me to stay with a friend of his called Brian for 3 nights. I met Brian outside Raynes Park station on Tuesday, March 14 and he didn't beat about the bush.

"I'm sorry to tell you this, mate, but you've got a killer illness and it's a killer illness that wants you DEAD..!"

As we made the short walk to his council flat, I got the feeling that this was going to be a drag. Brian was a chronic alcoholic, prone to relapses, but had been sober for a good while at this point and warned me not to even think about bringing booze into his house. His mother - whom he worshiped - had very recently passed away and Charlie evidently thought that the two of us might do each other good. He gave up his bed and hit me with both barrels of the AA/12 step manifesto for 3 days running, sharing his own disastrous history along the way. "You have the Gift Of Desperation," he told me, "And if you do the work, you'll be ok." I was still a little wary of renouncing my constant companion for the last quarter century but the seed had been sewn at the very least. When I left on a sunny St. Patrick's Day morning, I was committed to staying sober and might have done so had fate not conspired to take me on one last soul curdling drunken excursion.

That night, I met up with a friend in Earlsfield, hoping he would lend me some money to check into a hostel for the next couple of days. When that didn't happen, I bought a 3 litre bottle of cider and jumped a train from Kings Cross to Brighton. I had chosen this particular route because the service usually ran throughout the night but I arrived in Brighton just after midnight and found there were no outbound trains until 5am. Accepting that I was stuck for the duration, I sat on a bench inside the station and got talking to a young man who claimed to have been kicked out by his girlfriend. The upside was that he had a bottle of Southern Comfort and it wasn't long before we were sharing neat measures in the plastic cups that I happened to have in my bag. Another train pulled in and amongst the bright young things either concluding or commencing their nights on the town, I suddenly saw Boxing News scribe, Matt Christie, who was evidently returning from a show in the capital. Much to my embarrassment, he stopped to say hello. It constituted an awkward moment being recognised by a person of eminence from the world in which I had tried so hard to maintain a veneer of respectability. Our exchange was brief and polite but there was simply no positive explanation as to why I might be sitting on a bench after midnight, drinking Southern Comfort from a plastic cup with a ginger haired gargoyle. It was another nail in the coffin of my respectability.

I had vague recollections of trying to get into a nightclub with my unfortunate consort and then the next thing I remembered was waking up in a place called West Byfleet. I'd never heard of West Byfleet before and could only assume that it was located somewhere between Brighton and London. Clearly, I must have ditched my sidekick and stumbled onto a train in blackout at the crack of dawn. I spent another day and another night aimlessly riding the trains and downing enough cheap cider to anaesthetise myself from boredom and the elements before turning up on John's doorstep in Chorleywood on the Sunday evening. At some point en route, I had managed to lose my bag, meaning that I now had nothing besides the clothes I stood in. He let me stay the night but claimed to be expecting a plumber in the morning which necessitated my early departure. It was almost certainly a ruse to get me out of the house but I can't say I blame him.

On Tuesday March 21 at 10.30pm, I finally sank to my lowest ebb. Having managed to get hold of enough cash for 2 nights in the Boleyn Tavern at Upton Park, I stumbled into the Barking Road branch of Tesco's at 10.30pm and attempted to steal a 4 pack of Kronenbourg. I hadn't shoplifted in 2 decades and my ham fisted effort was duly foiled by an Asian security guard who exhibited a rage and indignation more appropriate to a man defending his Grandmother's heirloom. A scuffle took place as he tried to apprehend me but I escaped minus the beer and 2 buttons on my shirt. At that moment, even I had grown weary of this infernal madness. Spring had yet to kick in and here I was; the proud owner of a single shirt that would have looked more congruous on Tom Jones in the mid 1970s. I just couldn't do it anymore.

I drank 3 cans of cider the next day as a safeguard against withdrawal symptoms but took no pleasure in their consumption. Then on Thursday, March 23, I messaged my mother and admitted that things were worse than I had previously wanted her to know. Horrified to learn of the way I had been living, she sent £100 to Diana's account in order that she could pass it on to me but the handout came at a terrible price. I called at Maitland Road and received a severe dressing down from a woman who had come to view me as a lost cause and insisted that I stay away from Joseph and Lucas as I was no good to either of them. Before I left, she remarked that my protruding stomach might be symptomatic of liver damage and urged me to get myself checked out. The last few chapters have not been edifying but that was my real rock bottom: Being dismissed as a useless fat tosser and not even having the mojo to go back at her.

Many years earlier in New York, I'd heard it said that "AA is the last house on the block…" Feeling as if I had nowhere else to go, I avoided a drink for the rest of the day and rolled up at a meeting at the Dellow Centre in Brick Lane. I was too late for the tea making ritual and so took a seat in what resembled a brightly lit classroom containing around 15 other people whom I took to be alcoholics. Most of them looked pristine and healthy, quite at variance with the stereotype that a newcomer tends to hold. Something called 'the preamble' was read by an Eastern European lady before a cockney gentleman in a suit recited a confusing text allegedly known as 'The Doctor's Opinion.' It didn't make a lot of sense but I was in pain and if these people could make it better then the message could be in Chinese for all I cared.

I listened intently to the Scottish gentleman doing the chair and became engrossed in a story that held an uncannily soothing resonance. Like me, he had spent time in Paris and greatly enjoyed his drinking in days of yore. Over time, he had lost jobs and ruined relationships, blaming everybody besides himself and the liquid albatross that had ceased to be a drug of choice. Interestingly, he had been sober for 4 years at one time before dropping his guard at a christening and accepting a glass of champagne. 5 days later, he was face down in the gutter on a rainy night in St. Martin's Lane. By the time he was finished, I was a believer and wanted whatever it was that he and others in the room had.

"My name's Ben and I'm an alcoholic…."
At that moment the term was suddenly denuded of all shame and stigma. "Right now, I have no place to live, no bank account, no passport and the mother of my two beautiful sons has just

told me that I'm not allowed to see them anymore. I came here tonight because I want a new way of life. The old one doesn't appear to be working very well."

The meeting concluded with the serenity prayer and before I left a bespectacled man with an almost iridescent glow of well-being told me, "You're in for a glorious journey." For some reason, I believed him and hit the dark streets of Brick Lane feeling ridiculously optimistic about the future. I hadn't had a drink for 24 hours and didn't feel at all bad on that account.

Eager for more of the same, I went to a lunchtime meeting in Barking the next day and yet another in Bethnal Green that same evening. I had tried AA in the past and gleaned nothing besides the profoundly depressing sense that my life was over but this time around the same stories and teachings seemed hugely inspirational. For an alcoholic, getting sober has nothing to do with will power and everything to do with compliance. I had finally accepted that my thinking had achieved the square root of nothing and perhaps I didn't know everything. 48 hours sober by Saturday morning, I attended the big meeting at St. John's Church in Bethnal Green and received my 24 hour sobriety chip to a rousing ovation. For some, the courage required to walk 'on stage' was an achievement in itself but shyness had never been amongst my considerable failings.

'The Promises' state that our lives will improve beyond our wildest dreams 'sometimes quickly, sometimes slowly' if we faithfully adhere to the programme. For me, life improved radically in every aspect and in a way that I can only regard as miraculous. With the help of my younger brother, I was able to move into a flat share in East Ham and get a new passport. It was hardly a luxurious residence but I couldn't have been happier had I just acquired a lease on Buckingham Palace. For the first time in my life, I was truly grateful for everything I had, not least my health and sanity. Thanks to Brian, I also had a big smart TV and took great pleasure in catching up with the mainstream classic movies I had previously been too cool or distracted to watch. One of my flat mates was a volatile Nigerian alcoholic who would explode for no apparent reason but it just didn't bother me in this new mindset. The fellowship was teaching me not to worry about things beyond my control and merely to focus on improving myself.

Now my days began with a run around Central Park followed by a prayer and a bowl of porridge. The excess weight that I so despised was rapidly shed and friends began to remark that I looked 10 years younger. I had never really understood the concept of being 'high on life' before and the closest thing I could compare it to were those halcyon days of adolescence when everything seemed to reflect the charm of one's existence. I continued to attend several meetings a week, soaking up ever more knowledge of myself and the illness. I was very open about my recovery on social media and received fantastic support, alongside a blizzard of messages from people who were struggling with the booze themselves.

Within a matter of weeks, Diana relented and allowed me to see the kids again. She was never vindictive in that regard and had only been acting in the boys' best interests. Lucas was nearly 8 years old and our relationship duly blossomed now that I was fully present and not merely going through the motions of cosmetic parenthood. The so called simple things in life suddenly assumed enormous value and I discovered aisles in the supermarket that I had never previously been aware of. The wine, beer and spirits section had lost its appeal altogether. Boxing Social blew up and I was soon getting paid to attend pressers, weigh ins and promotions, although I stayed away from the Matchroom shows as I wasn't sure where I stood. Frank Warren was still not speaking to me but didn't seem to object to my presence at his events in a journalistic capacity. Perhaps my physiognomy had changed so much in sobriety that Frank just didn't recognise me.

I had been sober for almost 6 months when Mark encouraged

me to make my peace with Eddie Hearn. I should send an email, he suggested, apologising for my past conduct and asking for a reprieve. It sounded sensible enough but I had gotten to a point where my faith in a higher power was too robust to send a grovelling letter. "Everything will work itself out," I told him. "I'll see Eddie on neutral ground at some point, no doubt." Two days later I attended a press conference at the Landmark Hotel to announce a WBA Super Middleweight title fight between George Groves and Jamie Cox and Eddie happened to be there. I was surprised because it wasn't a Matchroom show but it turned out that Cox was a Matchroom fighter and the main man had come to represent him.

When I saw him on the dais, it was the first time I'd clapped eyes on Eddie since he had me ejected from the Sky presser, 14 months earlier. Knowing how much clout he had, I half wondered if a similar situation would unfold but I was evidently being a little paranoid. The principals made their speeches and questions from the floor were invited before the obligatory face off and one to one interviews. Having spoken to Groves, Cox, John Ryder and Kalle Sauerland, there was only one more notable scalp in the building. I wasn't going to ask him but my Finnish cameraman did and Mr. Hearn apparently had no issue with talking to the formerly notorious 'ticket gate thief' on camera. At the conclusion of a 15 minute interview, I requested that we take a picture, knowing that various people with access to my socials would be gutted to see us on friendly terms once more.

"I've made some changes in my life and haven't had a drink for 6 months." I explained. "I was wondering if it would be ok for me to come to the shows again…?"

"It's not a problem for me, Ben. Send Anthony Lever an email and I'm sure it will be fine."

Olive branch accepted, he was out of the chair and gone - probably en route to York Hall where he had a show that evening entitled 'Next Generation.' For the avoidance of doubt, I am not stupid or narcissistic enough to believe that the cameo I have just described constitutes anything more than an infinitesimal incident in the life of a future Hall of Fame boxing promoter. Nonetheless, for me it symbolised everything I had been encouraged to believe in the rooms of Alcoholics Anonymous. That no matter how badly a man fucks up his life, if he is prepared to get honest and take a fearless moral inventory of himself then he can - and will - recover. Further into the process, I came to realise that I couldn't ultimately care less if I'm in Eddie Hearn's good books or not. Happiness is an inside job and all the money and status in the world won't save a person who is suffering from the physical, mental and spiritual malady of addiction.

Having dispensed with the spurious concerns of status and popularity, I am left today with the things that I do care about. I care about staying sober and I care about being a good father. Above all, I care about my commitment to carrying out God's plan to the best of my ability. It's a commitment that I entered into unwittingly on March 23, 2017 and - more than 4 years down the line - I haven't touched a drop of alcohol since. God is a word that causes many an intellectual to start frothing at the mouth as he attempts to beat you down with science and reason. Some have drank themselves to death rather than entertain the notion that a Divine Being could restore them to sanity. But f it was a belief system that got me sober then let me hereby count its tenets:

I believe in adhering to a consistent ethical value base that includes apologising when our actions fall outside of it. In such cases, I believe in making amends where possible.

I believe in energy and the concept of action and reaction. I don't believe that everything in life happens purely at random.

I believe in being true to yourself and doing the right thing and I believe in letting go of resentments. I believe if you stay on that path and give it your best shot then happiness and contentment will follow, even if it seems like a long game at times.

Crucially, I believe that Evil will always destroy itself in the end and Good will be exonerated.

And I believe in gratitude. Accordingly, I am grateful to you for persevering with this ragged story and making it to the end. Ironically - for me - life is just beginning.

EPILOGUE:

An alcoholic will never realise his true potential until he puts down the drink, no matter how much he may achieve while lingering in the madness. I talked about writing a book for years but progressing beyond a few chapters required a focus and patience that I just didn't have when I was drinking. I'd always believed that booze and drugs served as elixirs making us better able to create art and appreciate the true wonder of life but, in my case, the evidence suggested otherwise. My world needed to get very dark and narrow before I was able to see the light and it was never going to happen before every alternative avenue had been explored. I have no interest in lecturing the harmless social drinker and neither do I have a problem being in his company but, still, I'm amazed how agreeable life can be in one's straight head with the obsession removed.

I have a lovely home today for which I'm truly grateful, in contrast to the era when I regarded people who got sentimental about bricks and mortar as braindead suburbanites. I have a gorgeous girlfriend and our relationship thus far has been totally devoid of the drama and toxicity that marred pretty much every other romantic liaison of my life. Most importantly, I have 2 beautiful sons who actually want to spend time with me now that I'm not under the perpetual influence of a drug that might have already killed me had I continued down the road I was on.

I don't know if I'll ever drink again but I do know that I won't drink today and also that I haven't fancied one in a long time. To be precise, a google search informs me that I have been sober for 1577 days at this time of writing. Of those 1577 days, only one of them could be described as a certifiably bad day from my perspective and only then because I had a chronic toothache and Marvin Hagler died. No doubt worse things will happen in the future as that is simply the nature of life but - however much time I have left - I would like to see mine through open eyes from here on in.

As a wonderful old boy who frequents the Canning Town meetings is fond of saying: "Growing old is mandatory. Growing up is optional."

It's been a long, hard road but if I can do it then anyone can.

ABOUT THE AUTHOR

Ben Doughty

Ben Doughty is a boxing, coach, journalist and pundit who resides in London. He has two sons, a cult following and an army of detractors who probably need to get out more. He has pledged not to write anymore books about himself.

Printed in Great Britain
by Amazon